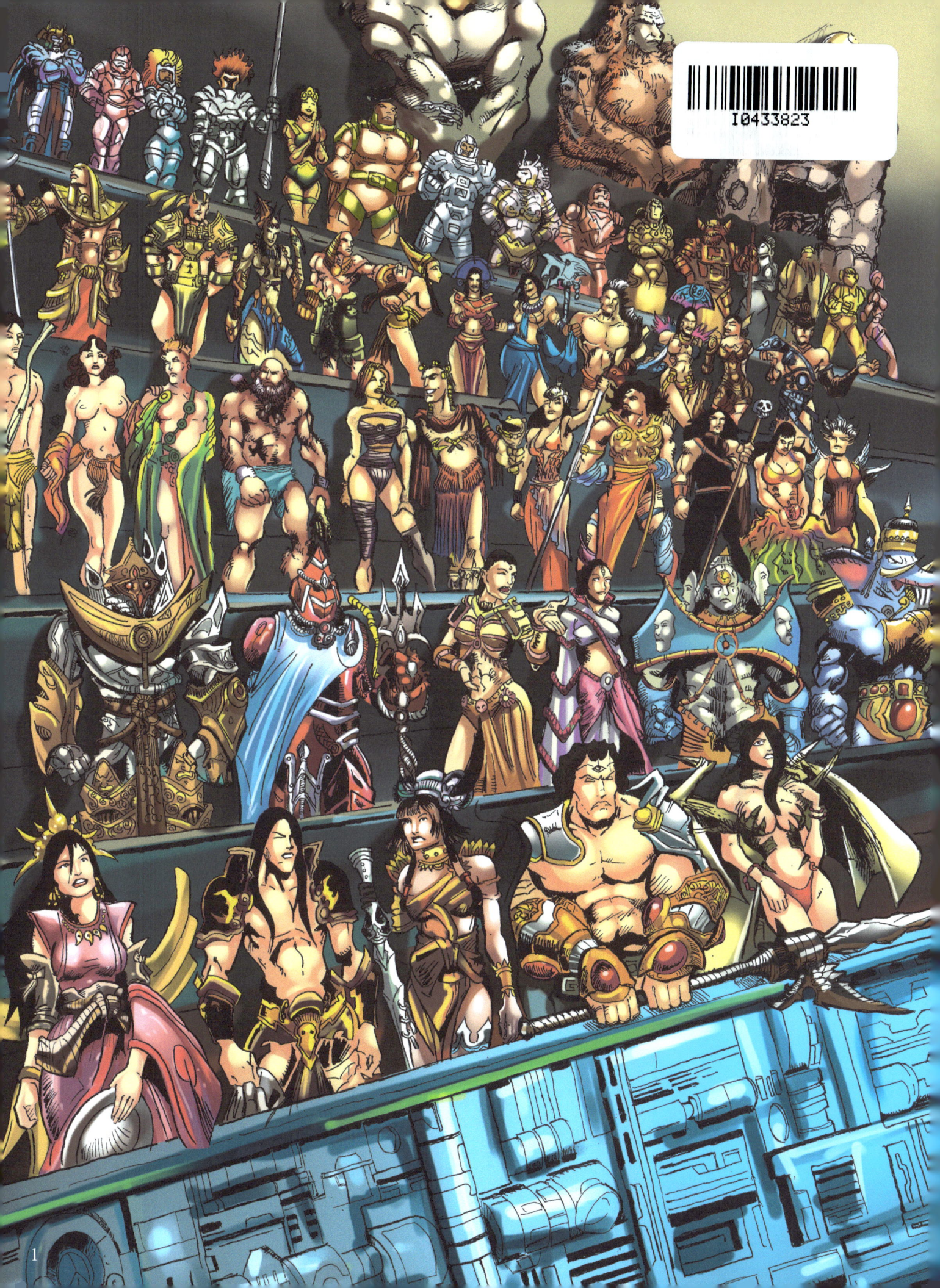

The Art of Pantheon
Copyright © 2018 Awet Moges

All rights reserved. No part of this work may be reproduced or transmitted in any form or by any means, electronic or mechanical, including photocopying, recording, or by any information storage or retrieval system, without the prior written permission of the copyright owner and the publisher.

This is a work of artistic fiction. Images, characters, businesses, places, events and incidents are either the products of the artist's imagination or used in a fictitious manner. Any resemblance to actual persons, living or dead or fictional, or actual events is purely coincidental.

Printed in United States of America

Publisher
Pood Paw Prints, LLC
https://www.poodpawprints.com
https://www.facebook.com/poodpawprints

Press information:
thorson@poodpawprints.com

ISBN-13: 978-1-944854-05-8
ISBN-10: 1-944854-05-3

Cover Art
Awet Moges
awet@poodpawprints.com
Interior pages 1-49,52-53, Awet Moges
Interior page 50, Marianovella Sinicropi
Interior page 51, Nicole Serra

Other works by Pood Paw Prints:

Pantheon: Heterotopia
The Pood: Michigan's Inferno
Abe 2.0: Welcome to the Asylum, Mr. President

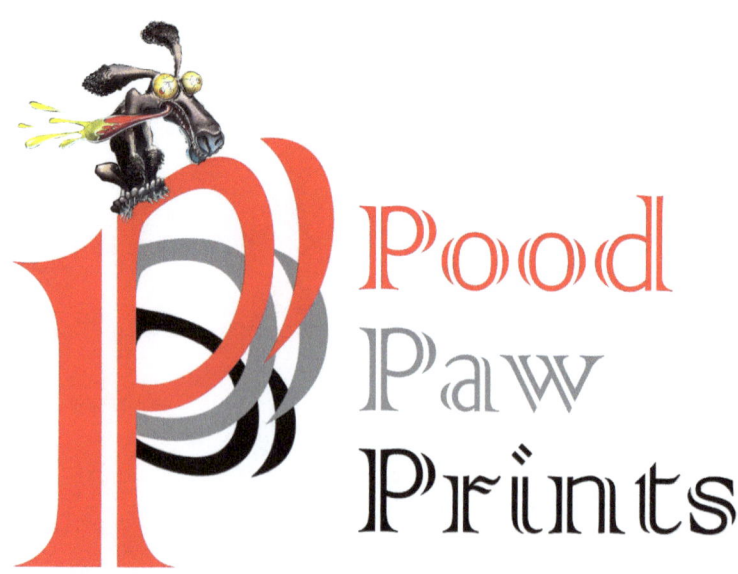

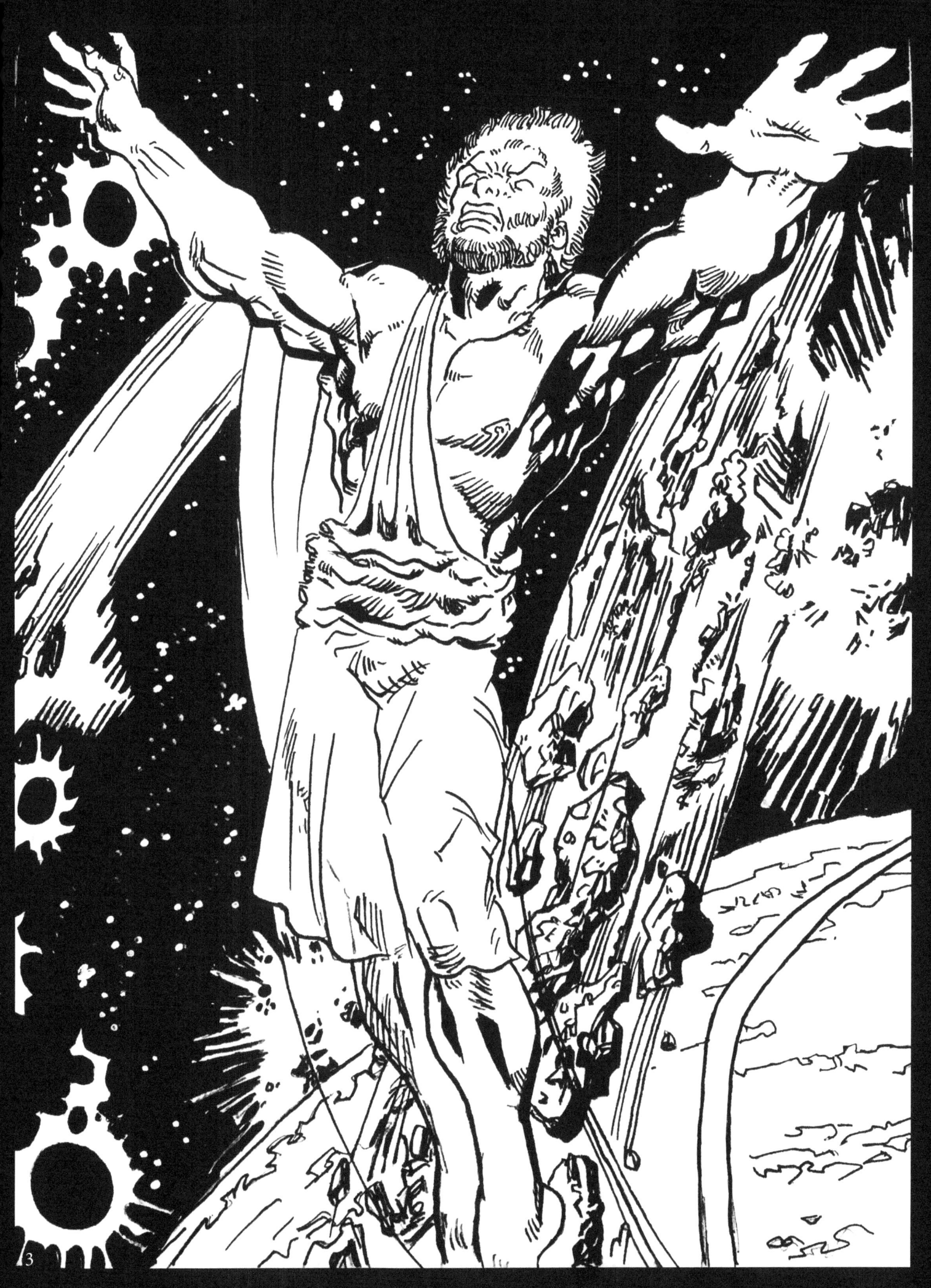

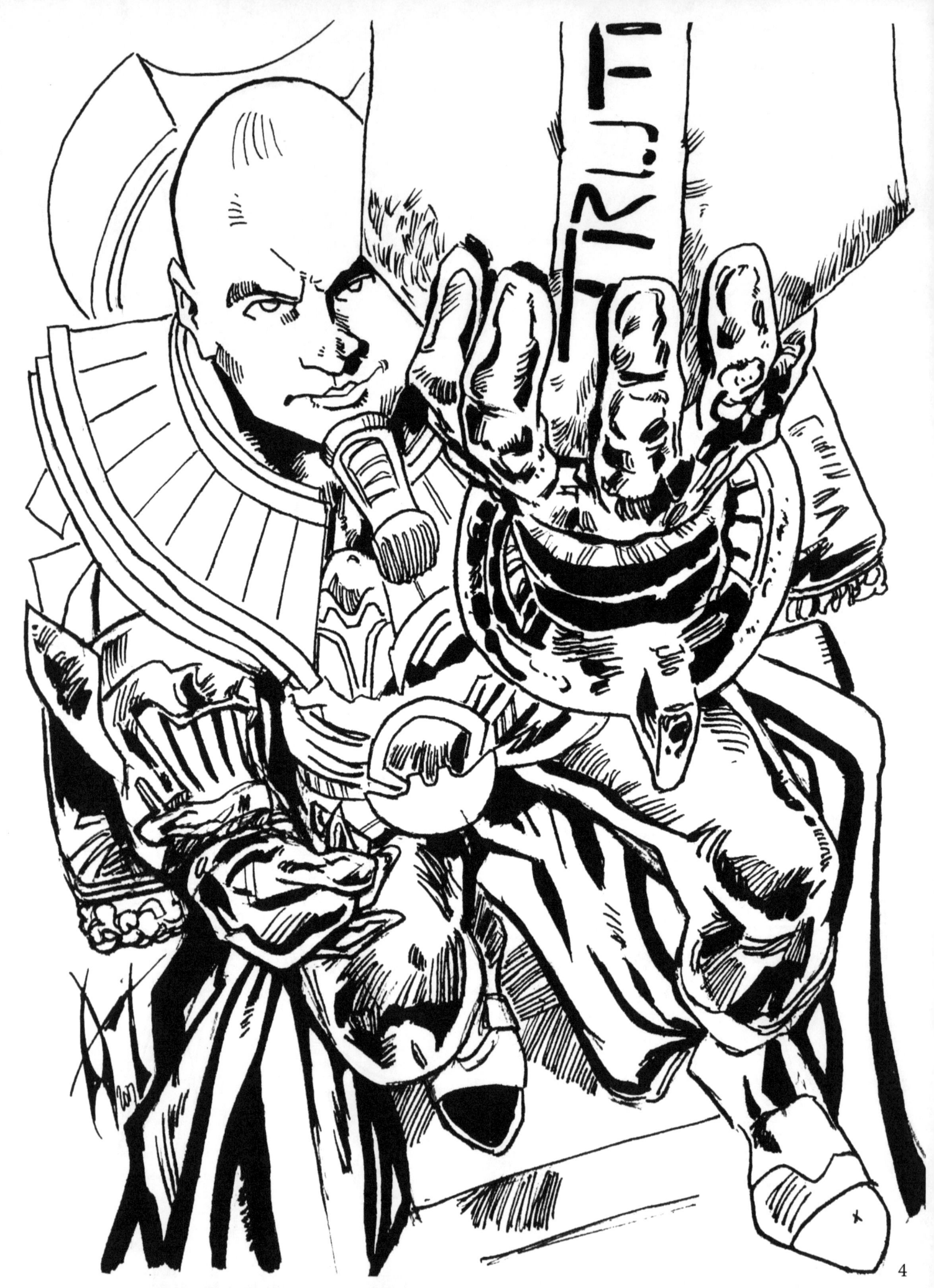

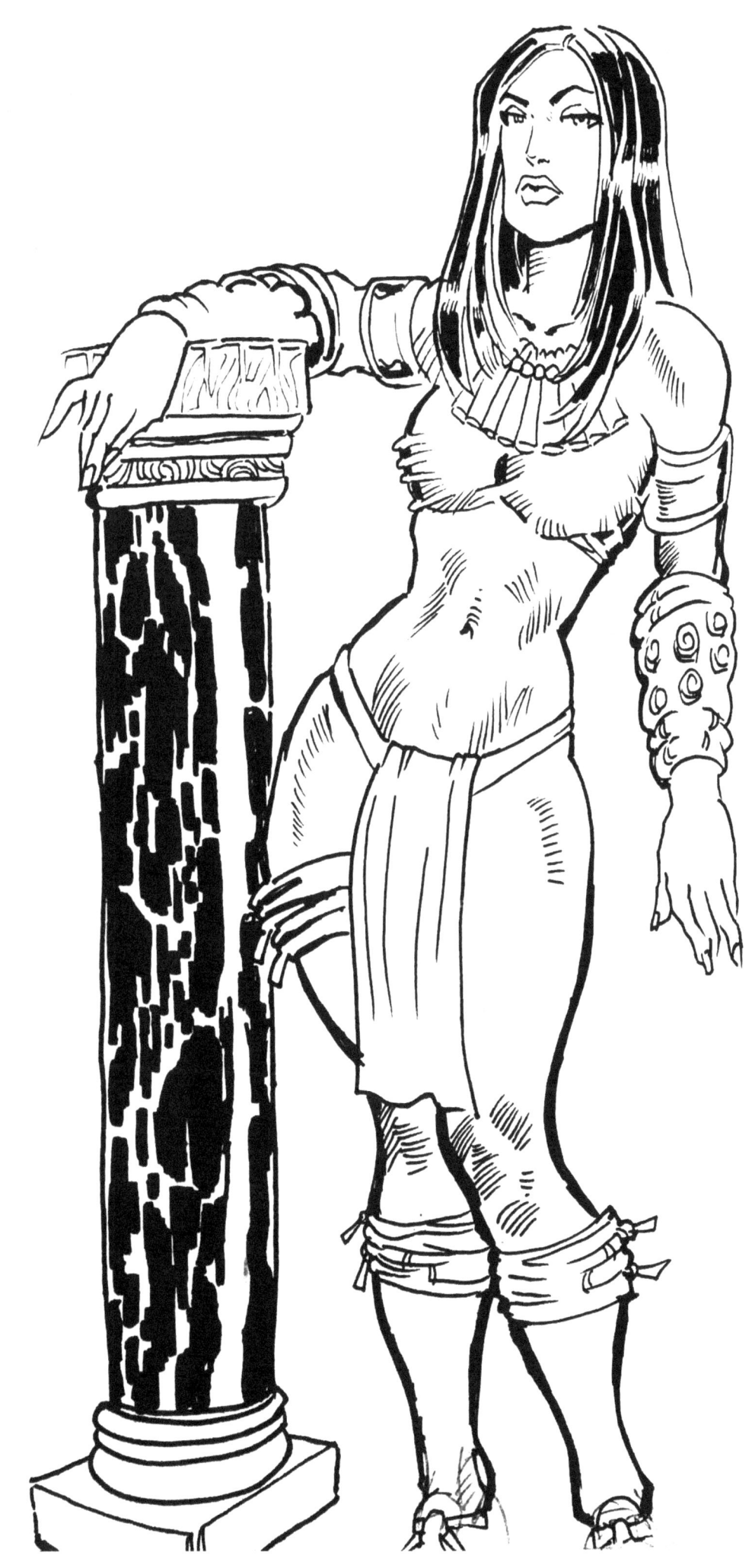

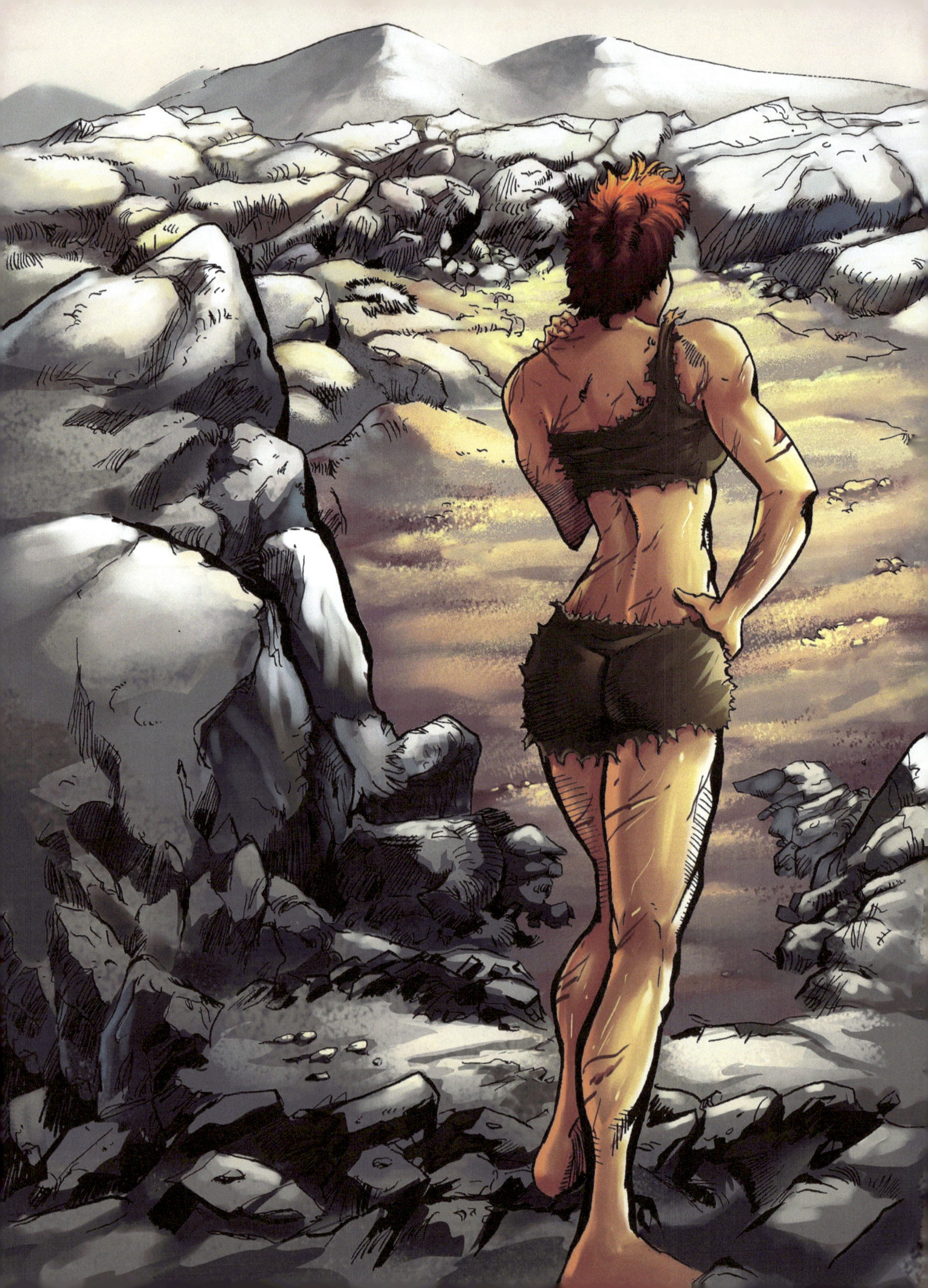

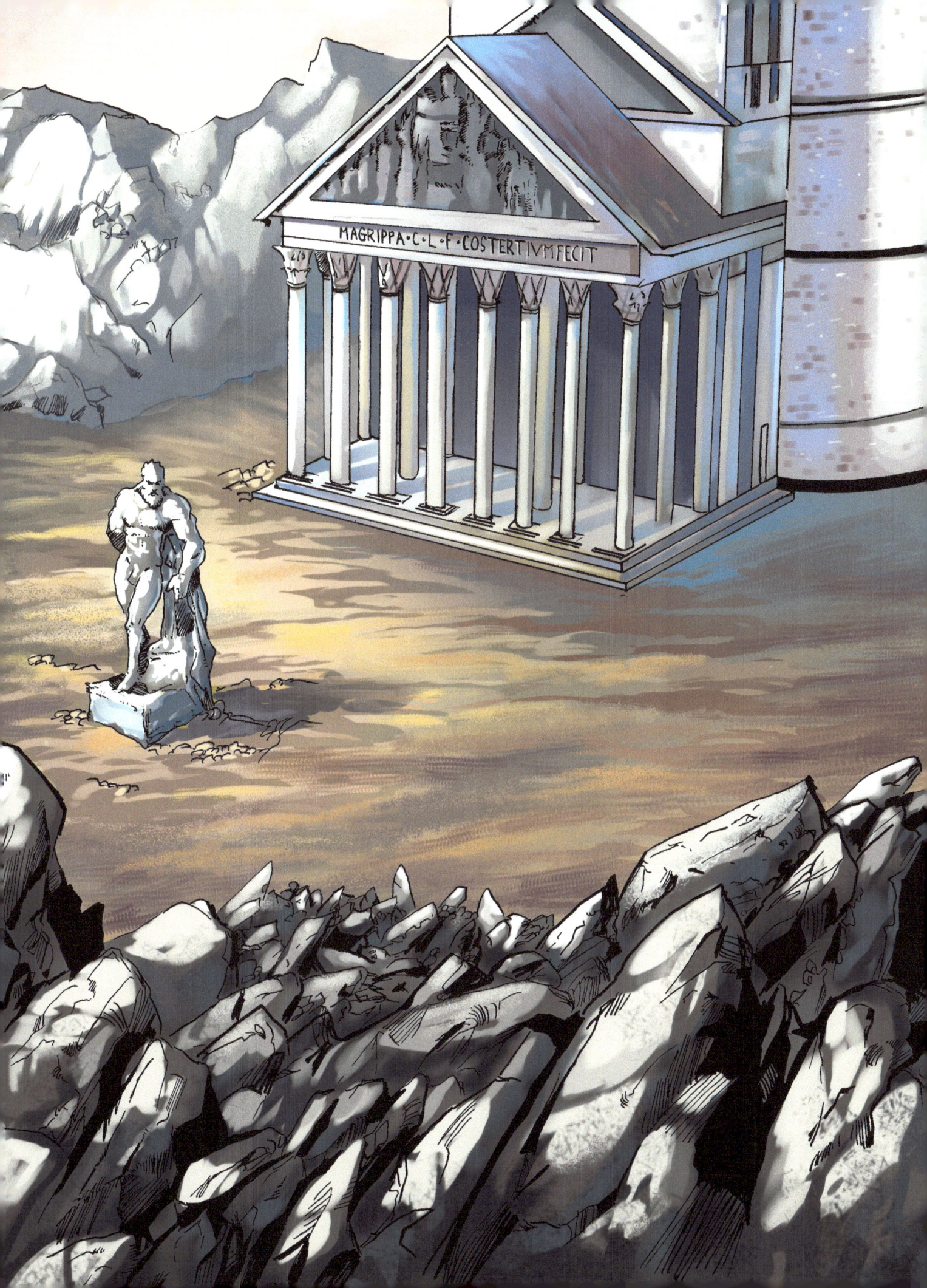

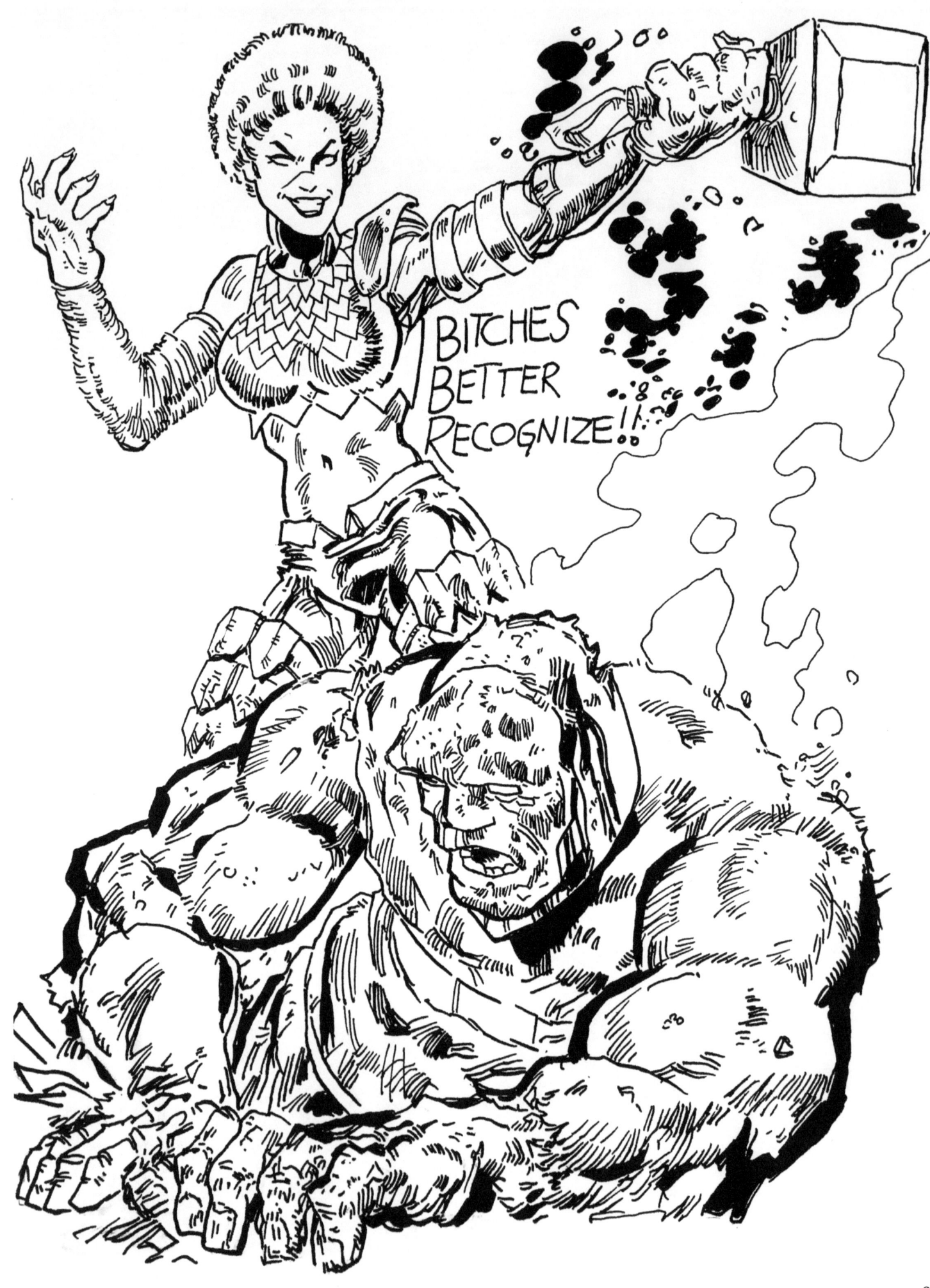

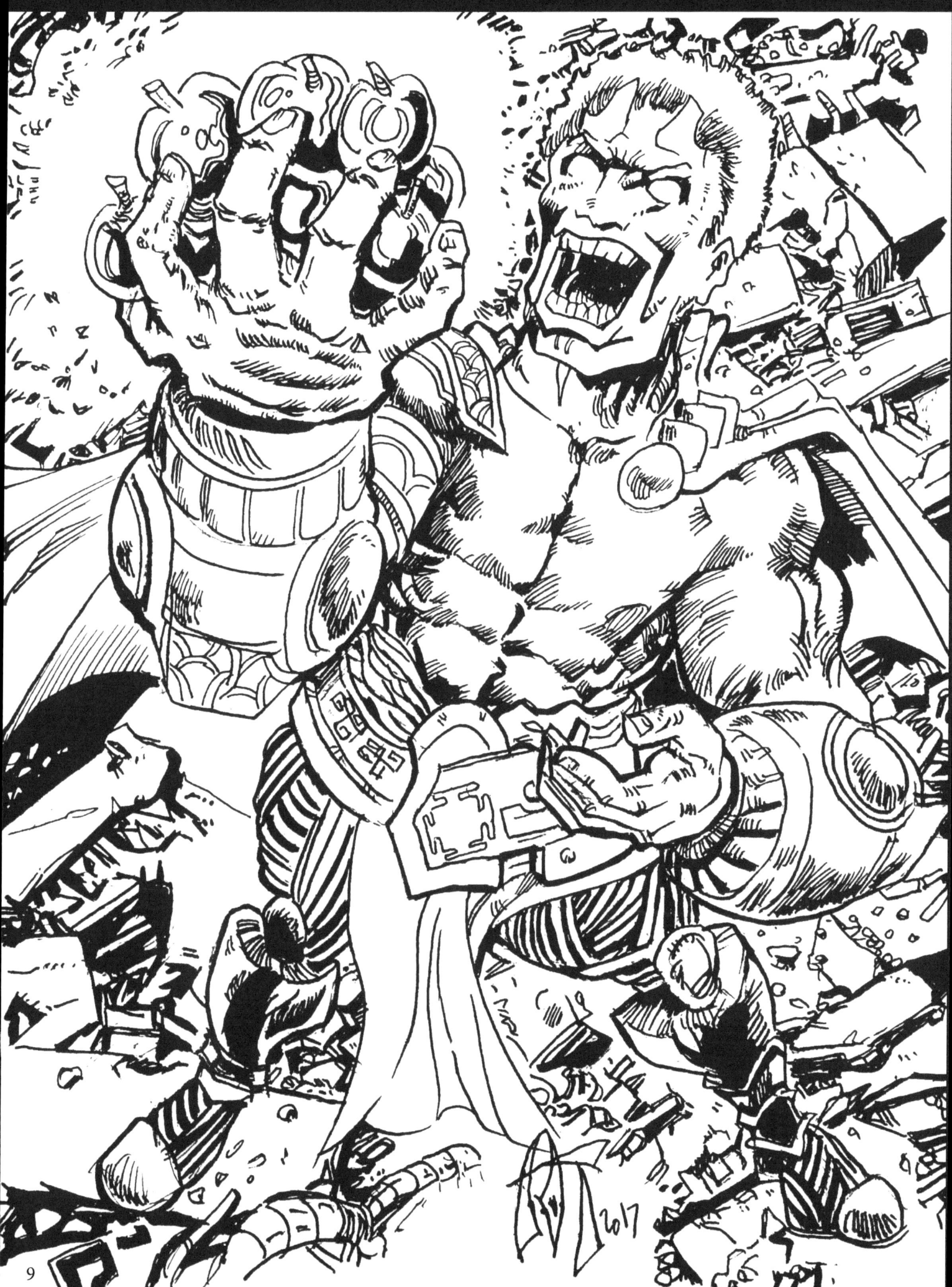

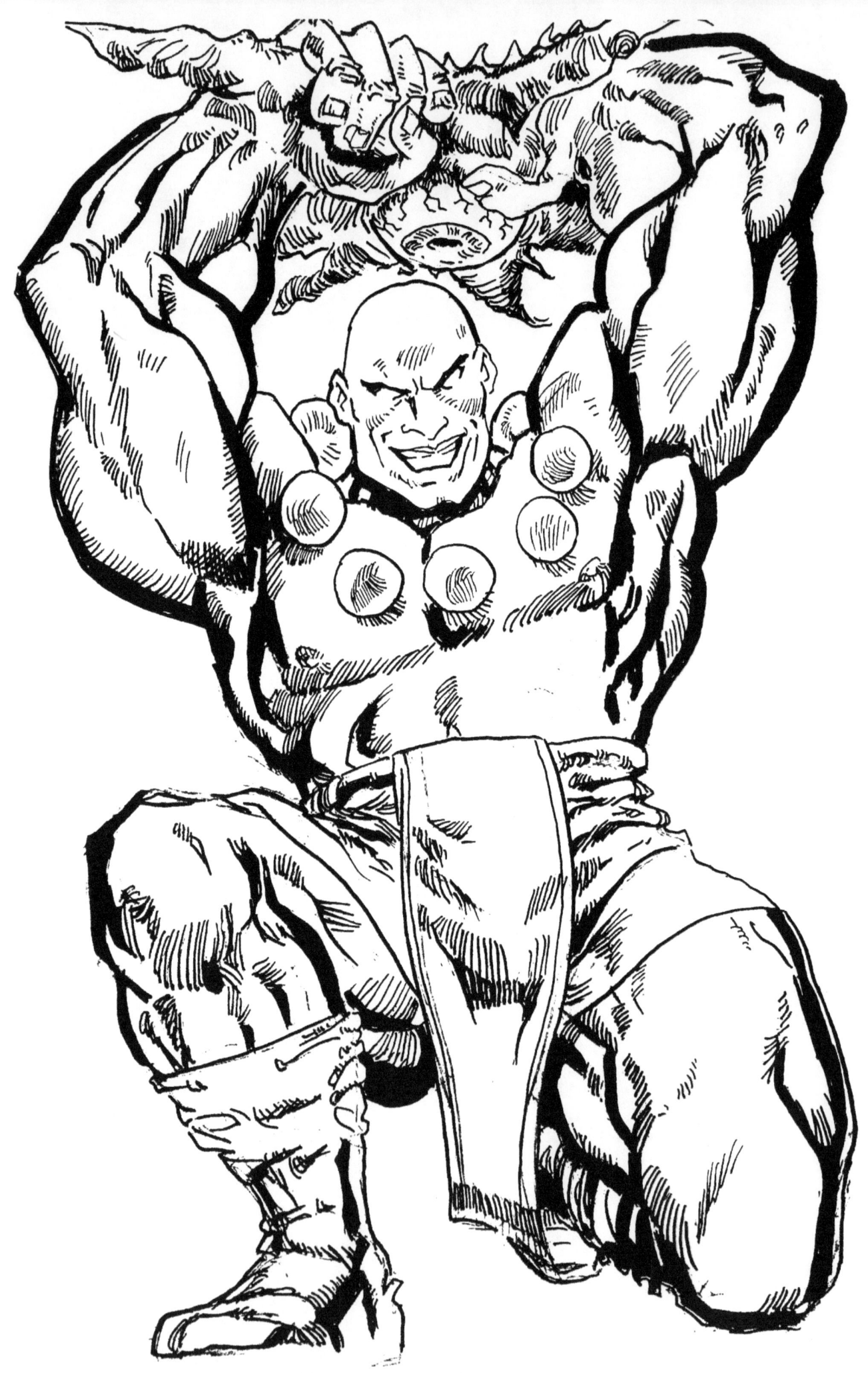

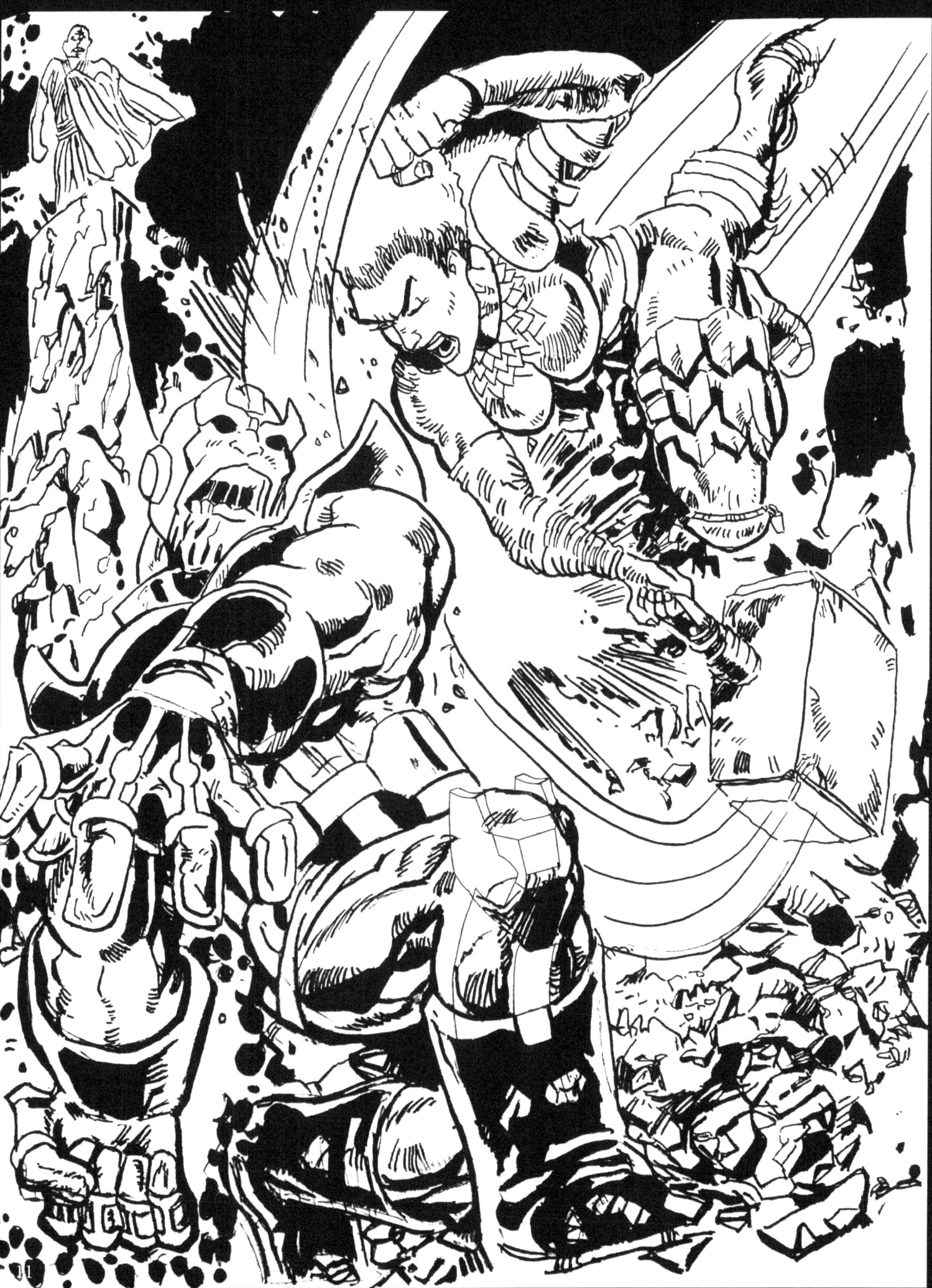

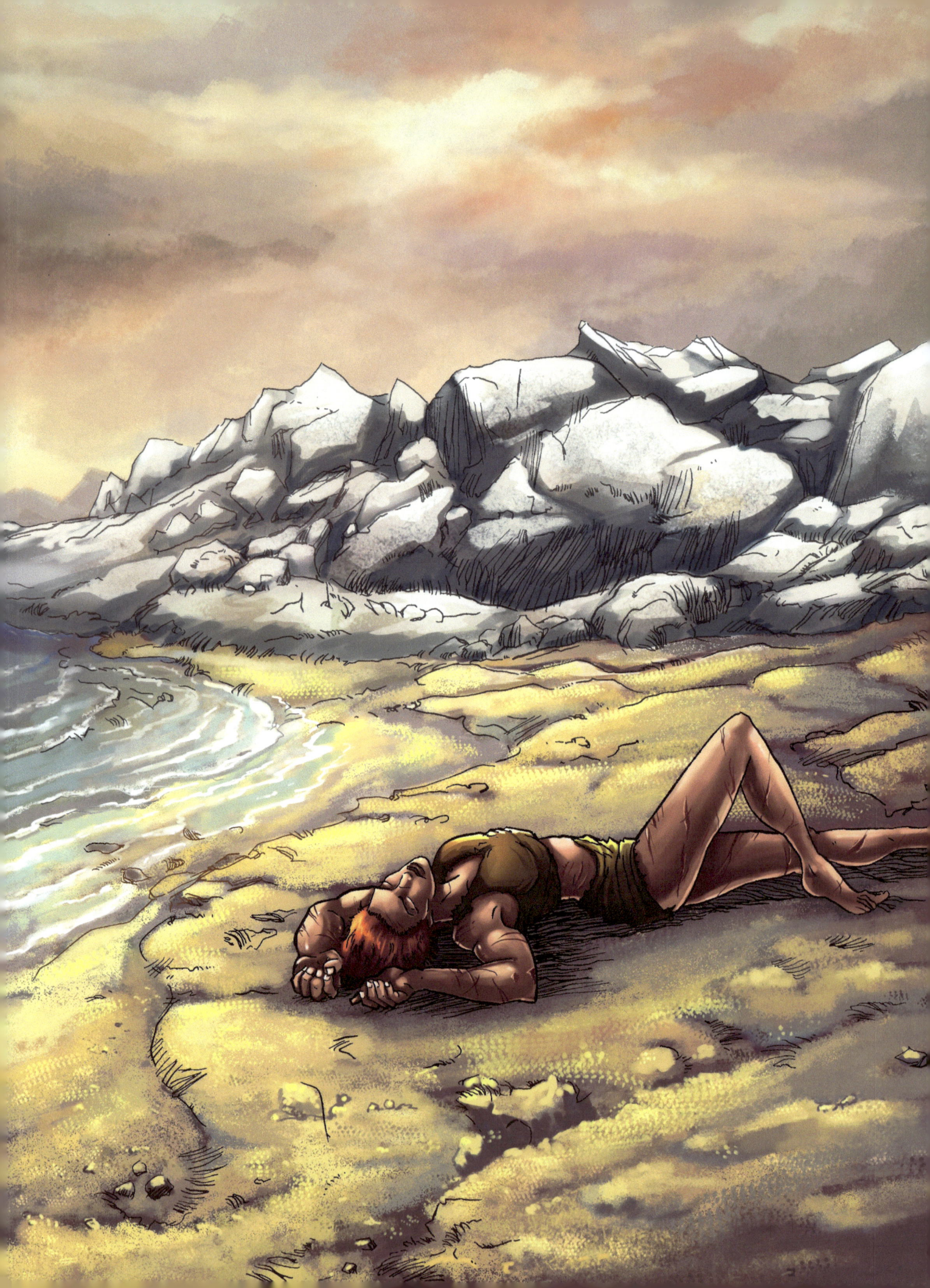

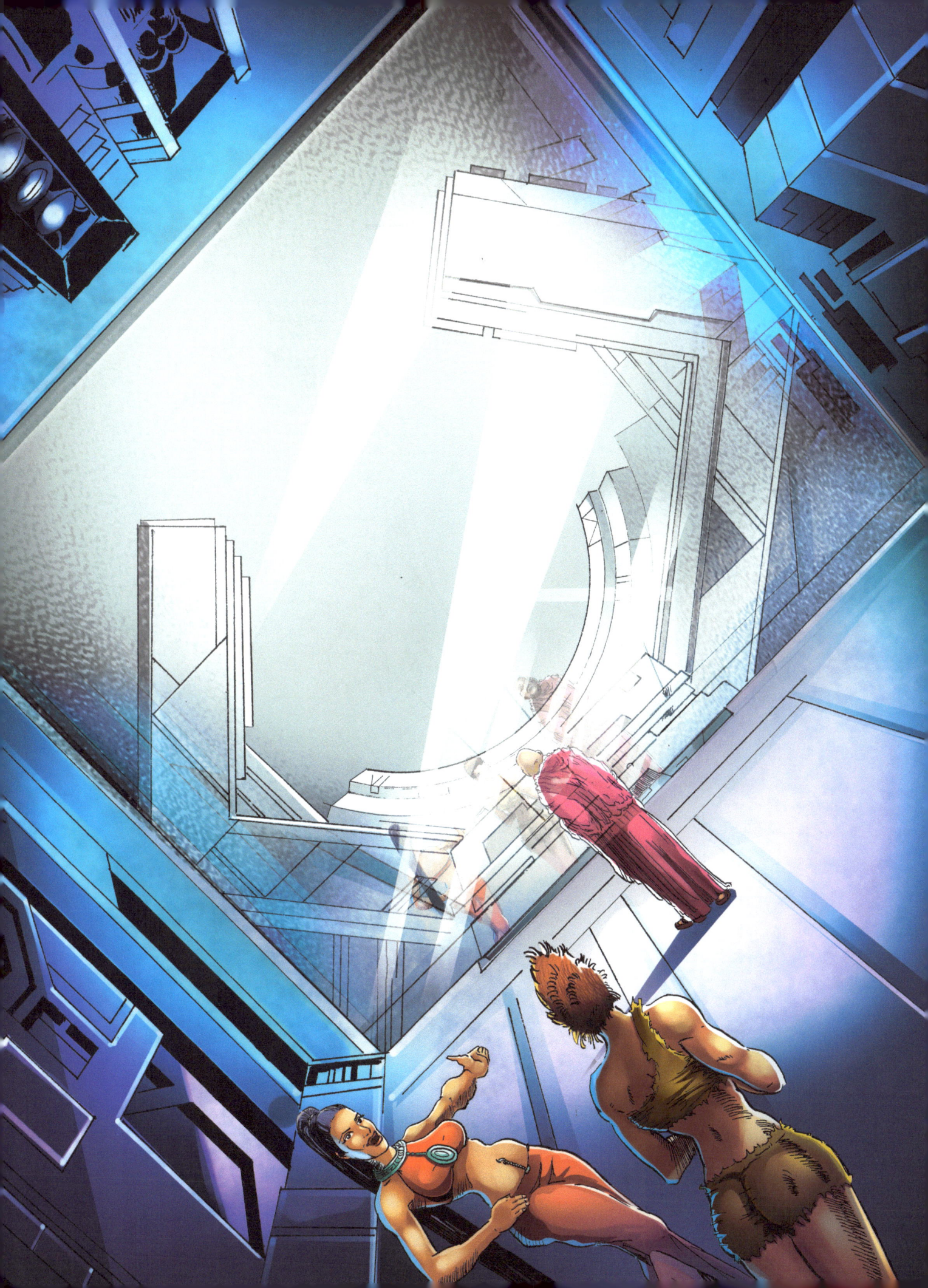

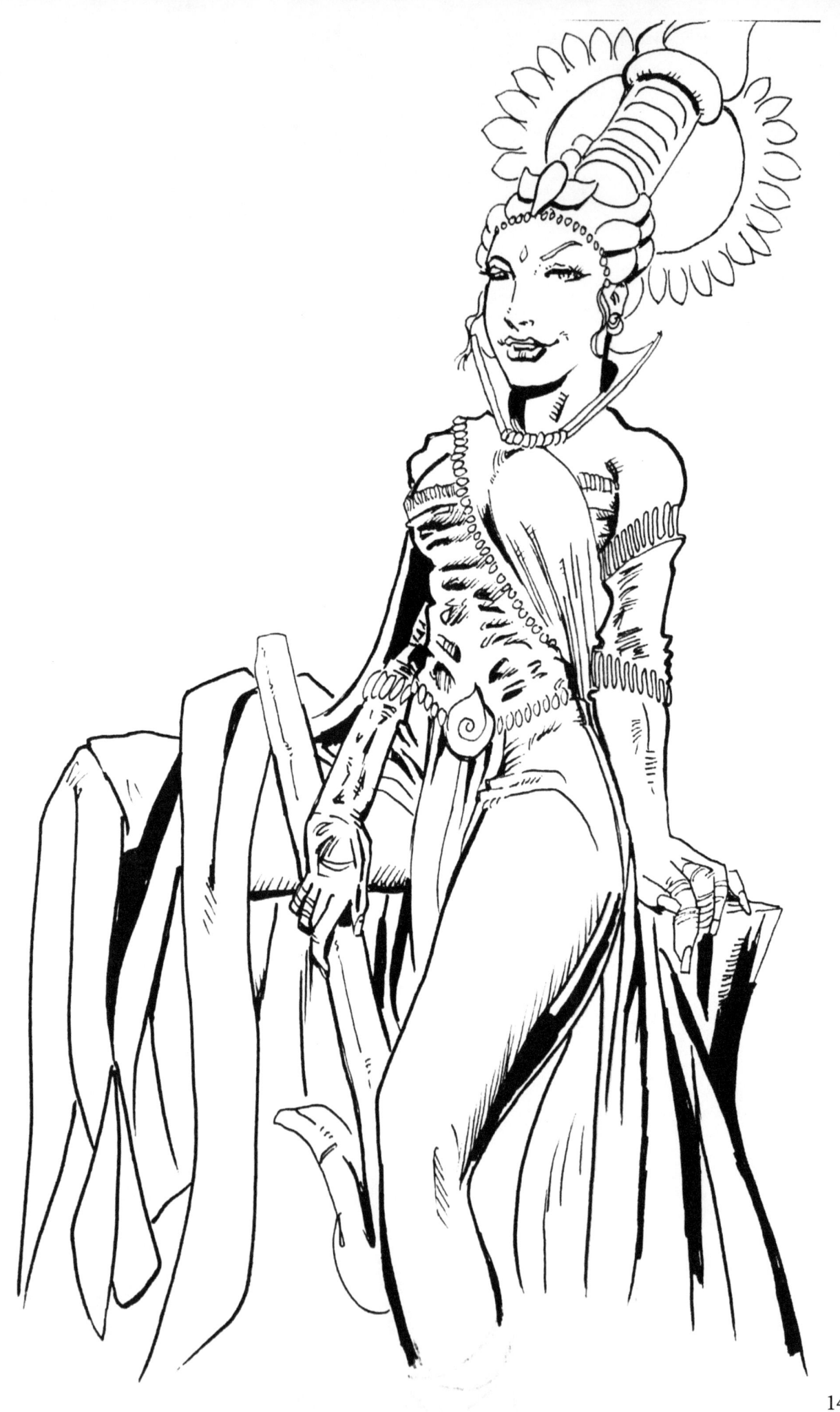

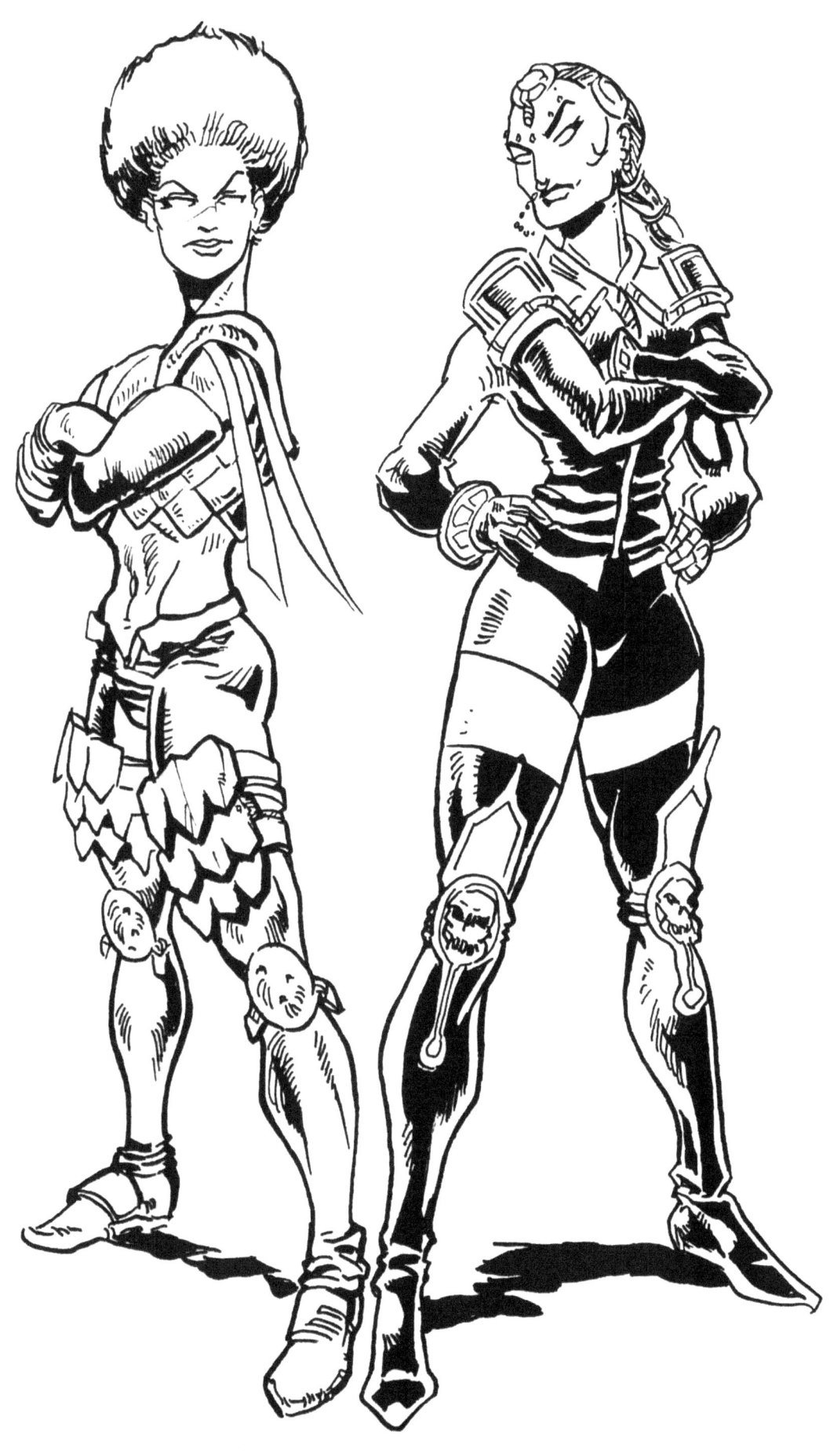

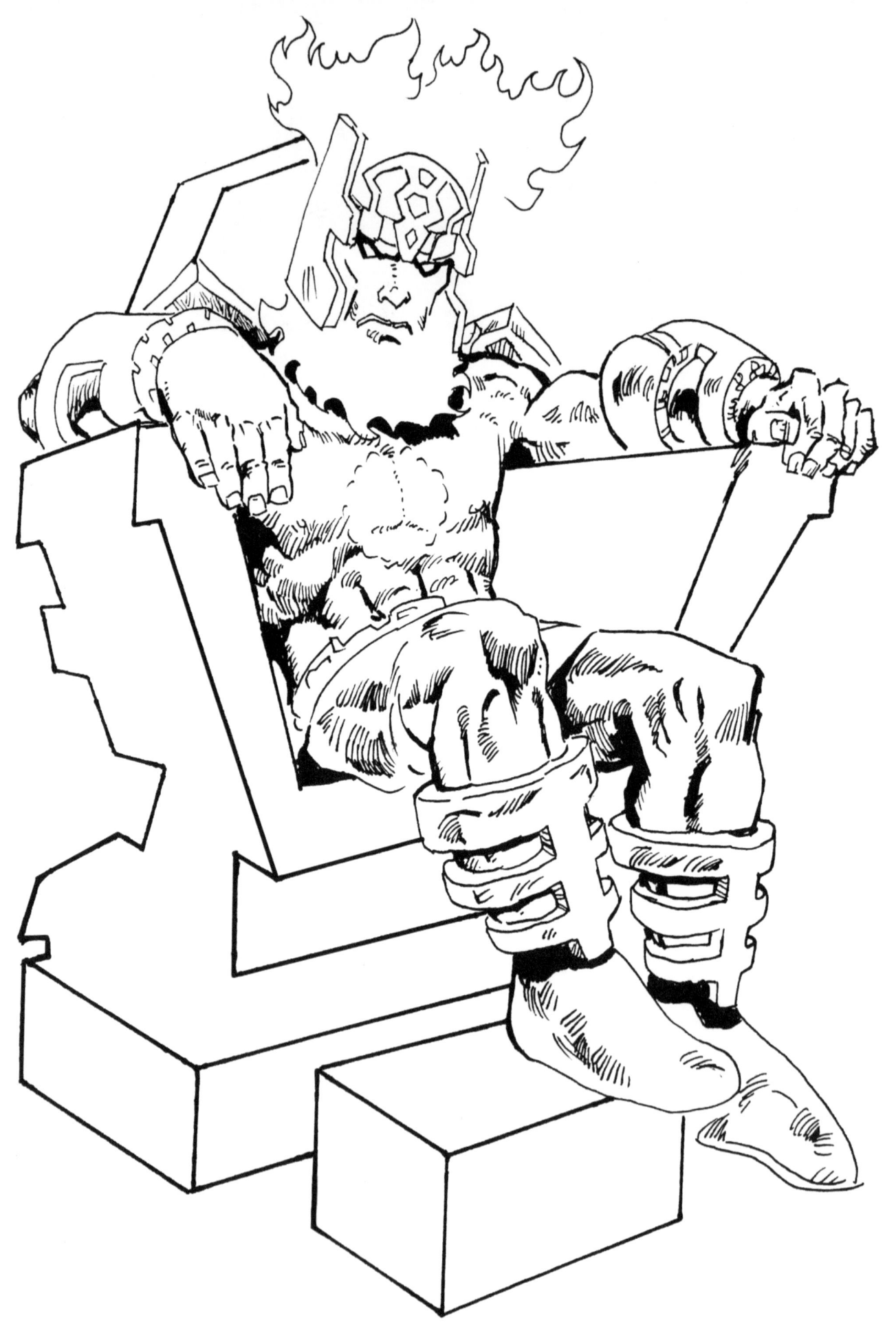

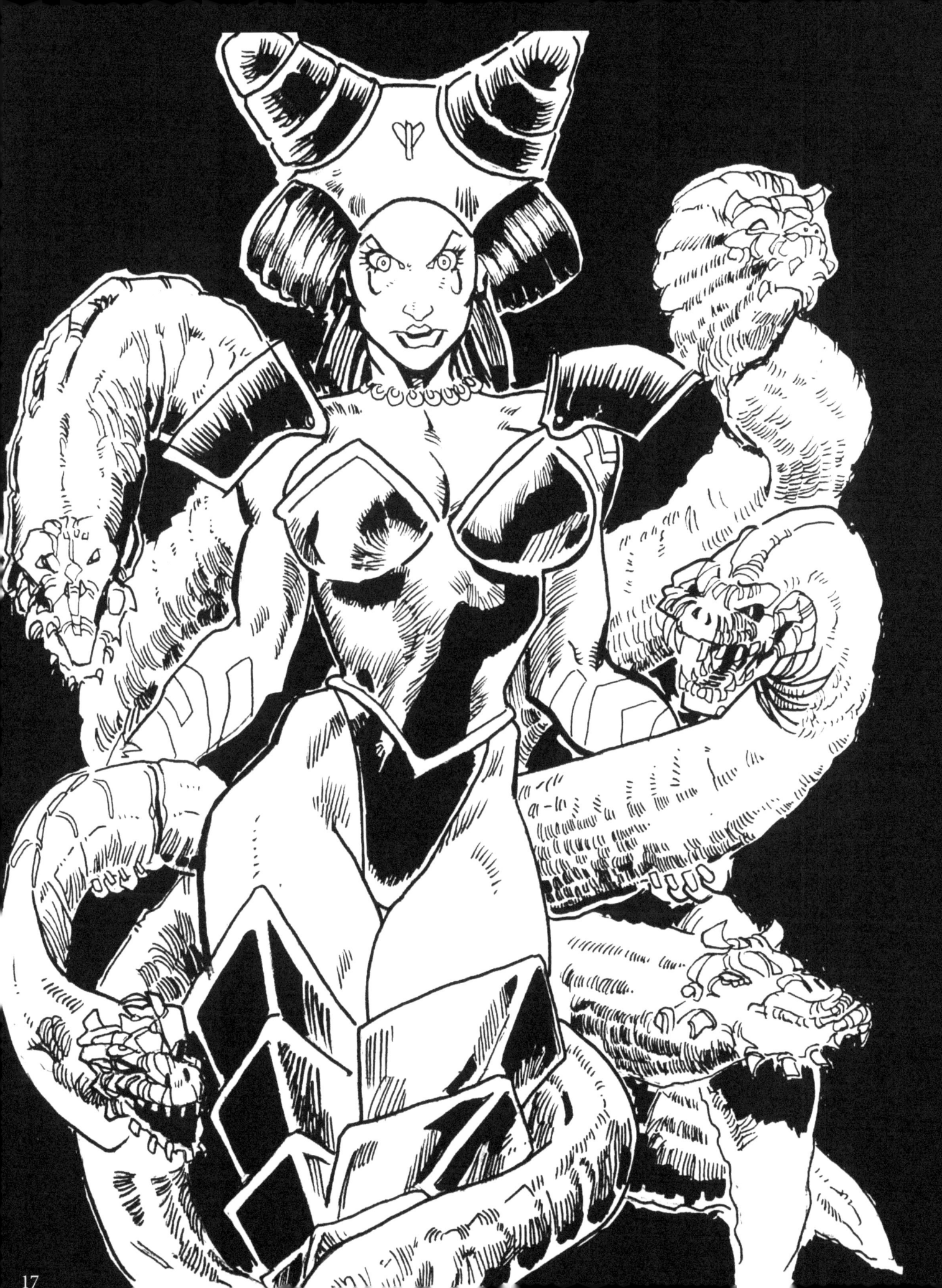

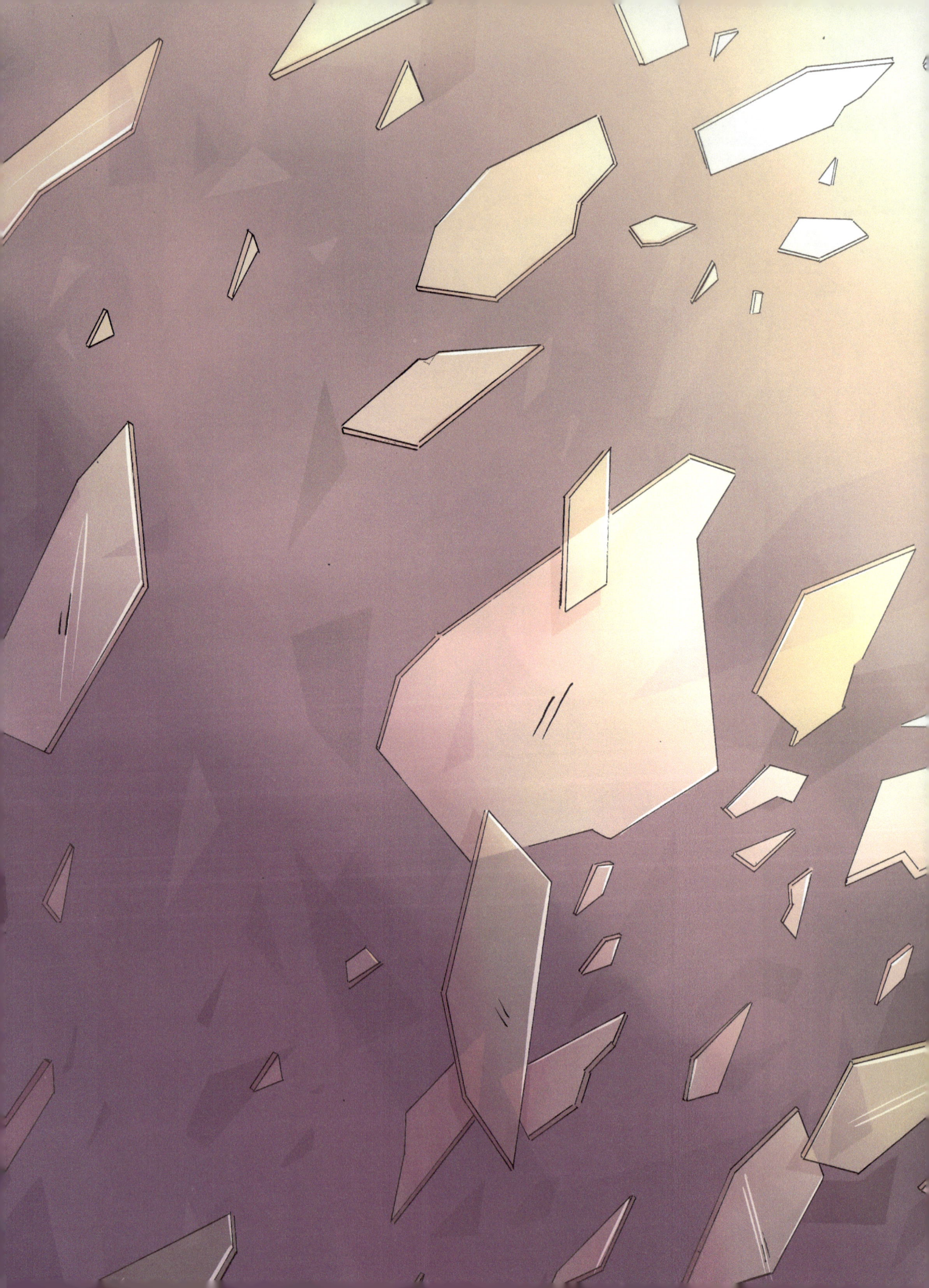

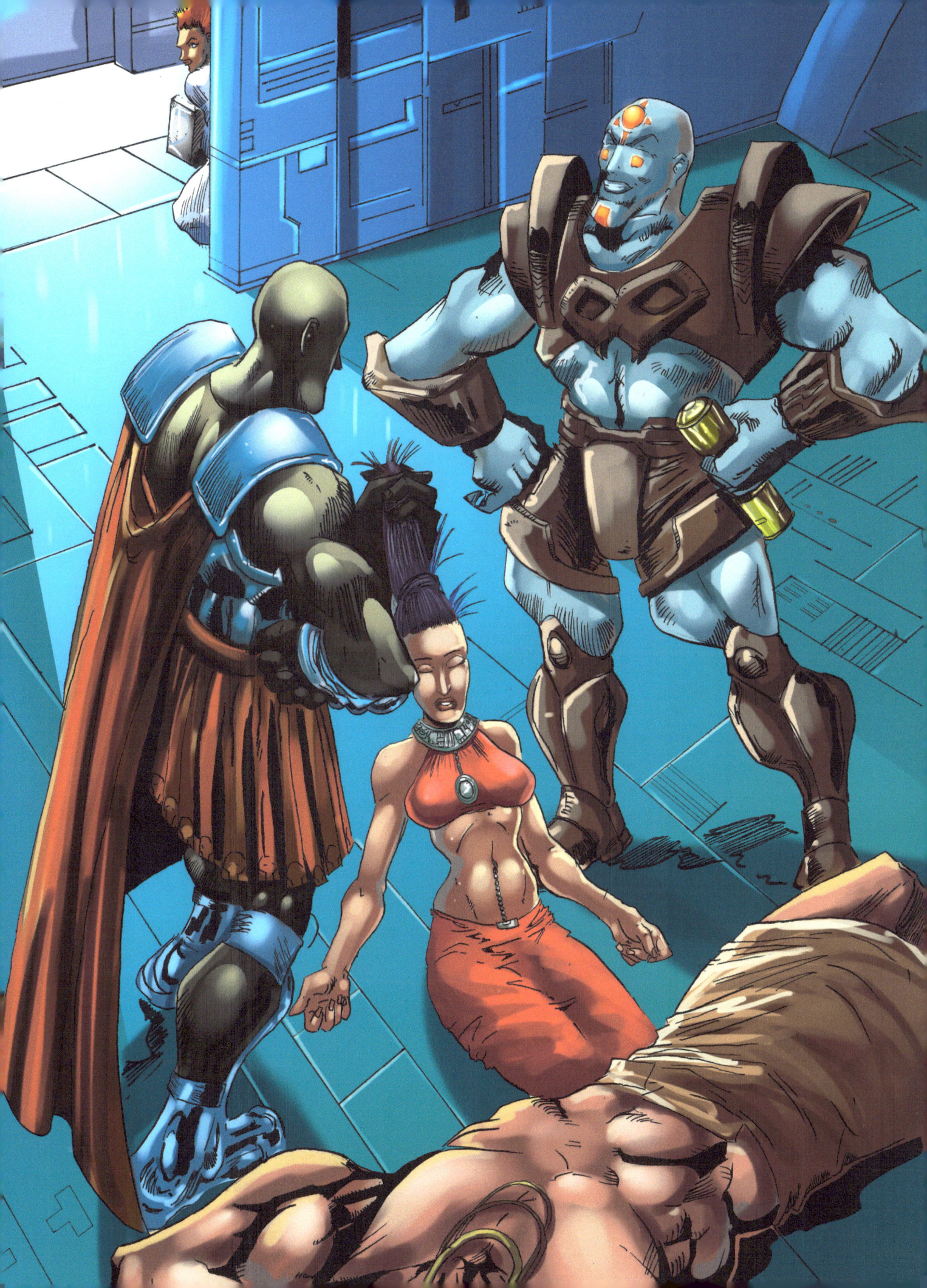

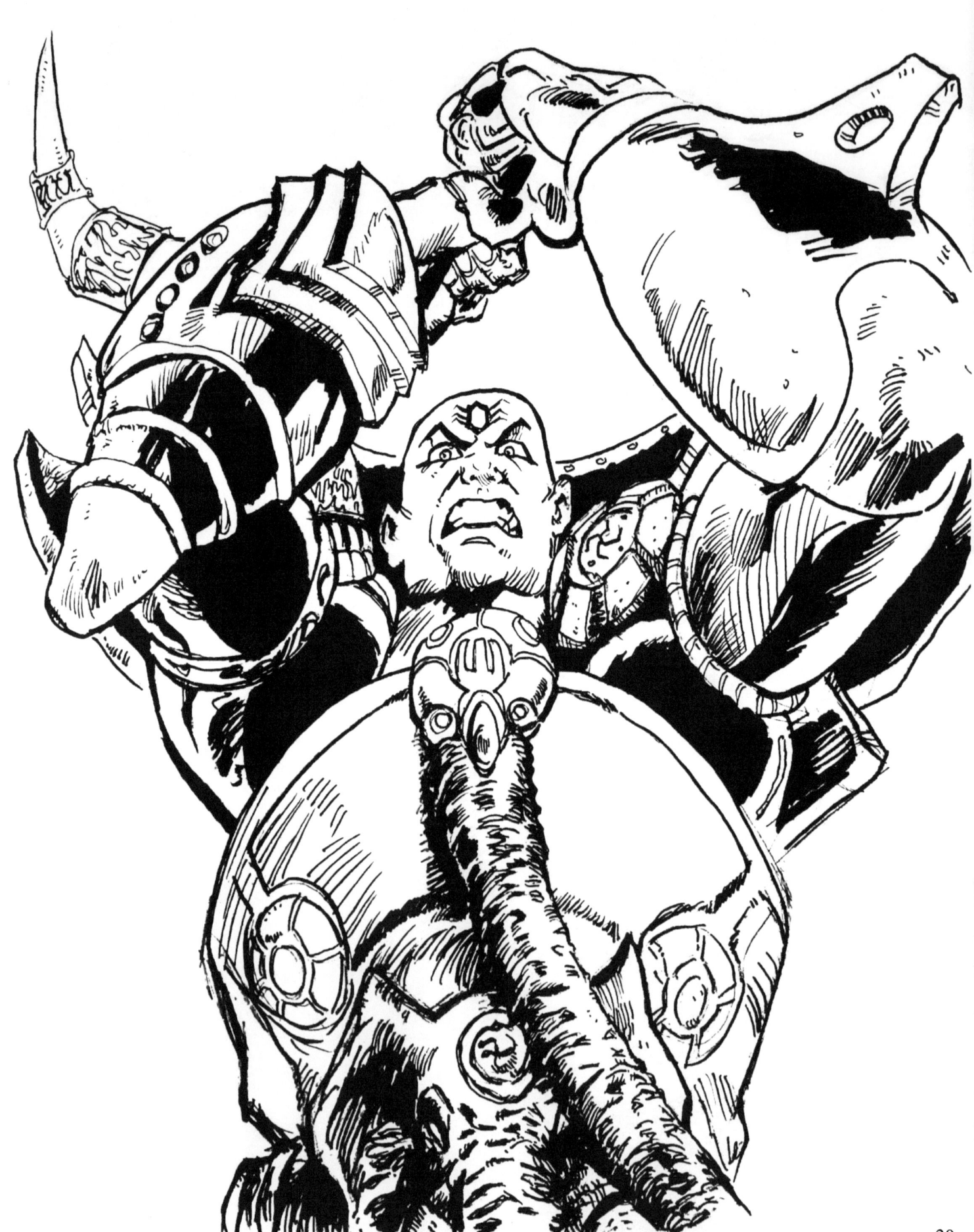

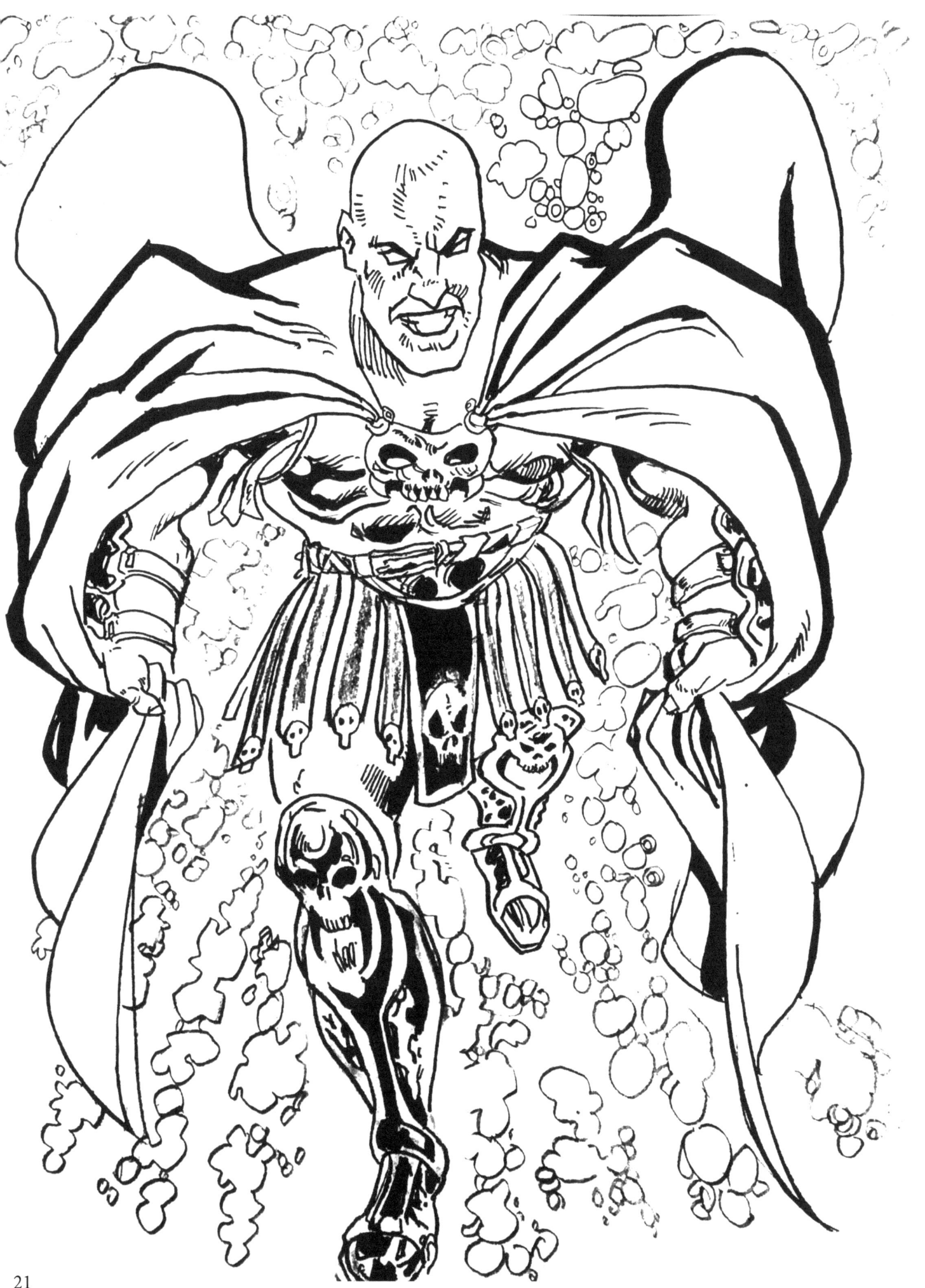

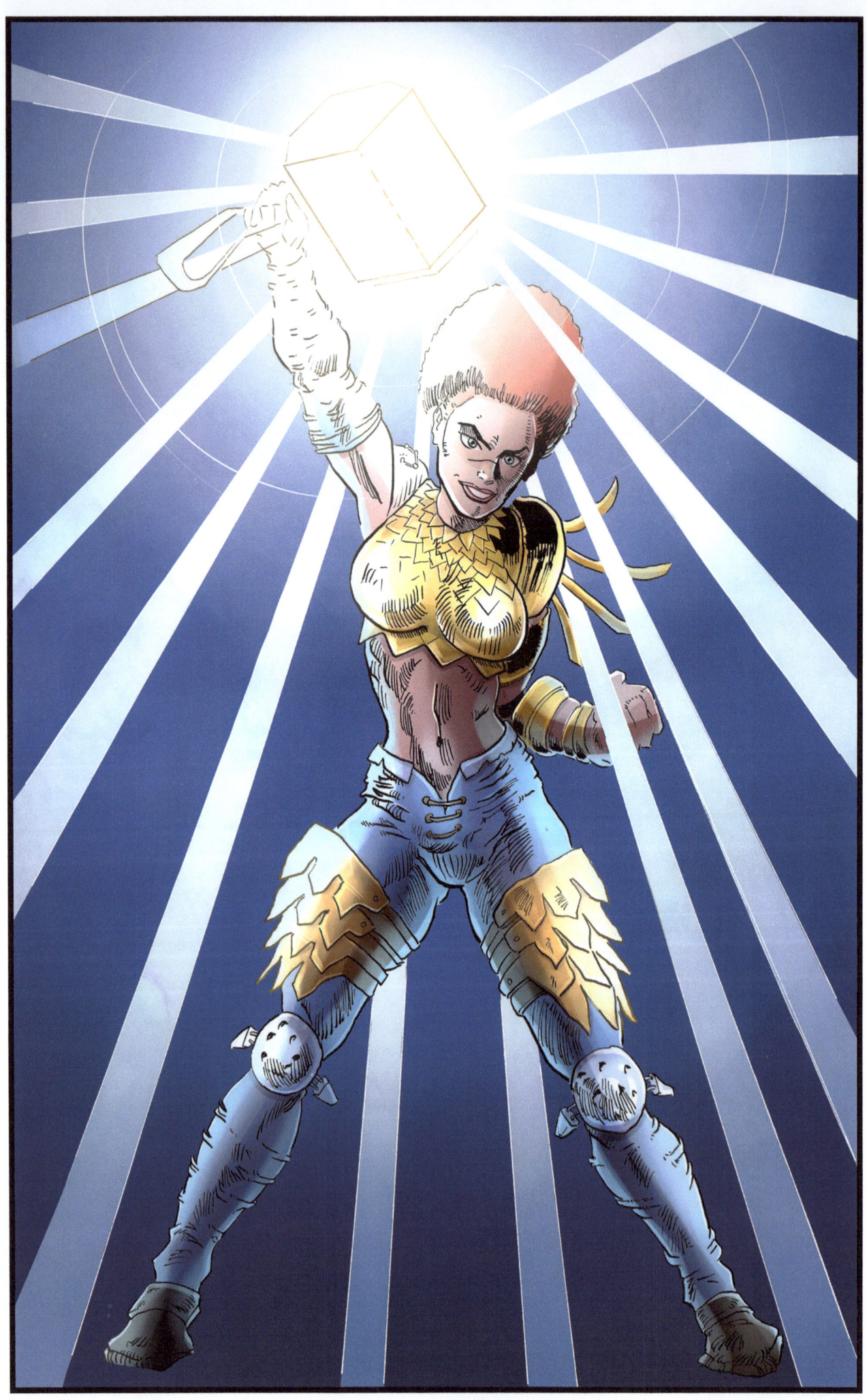

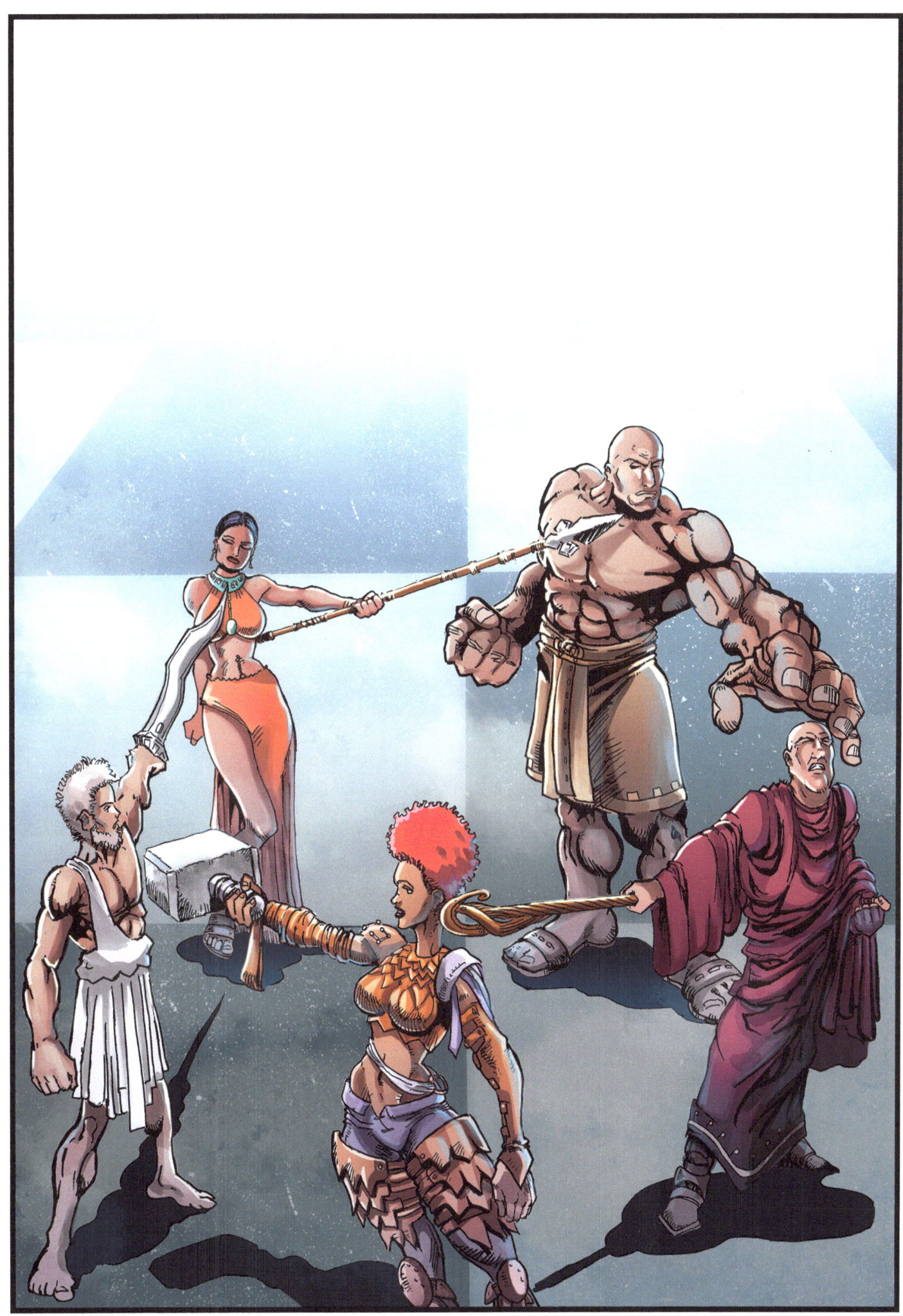

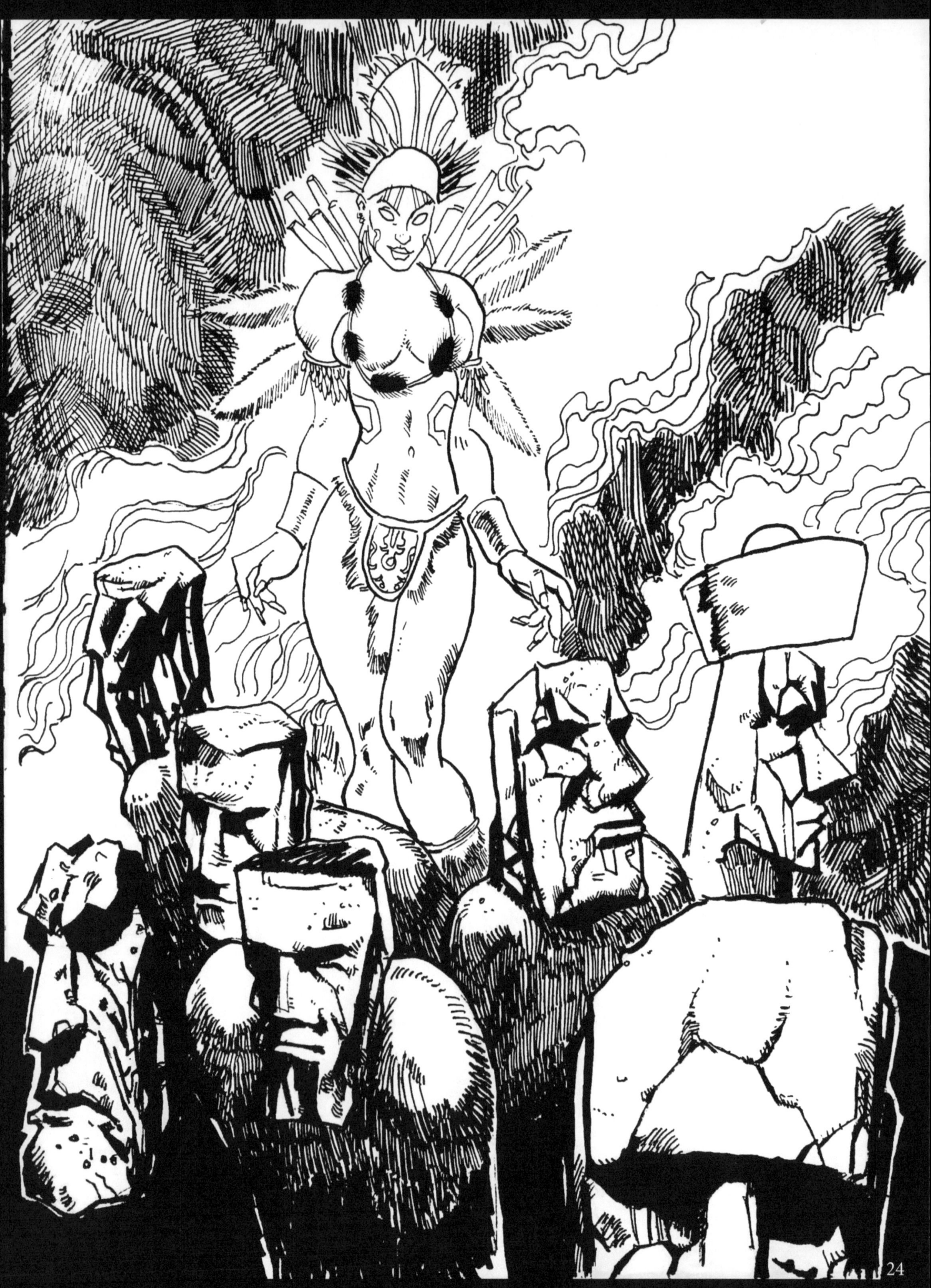

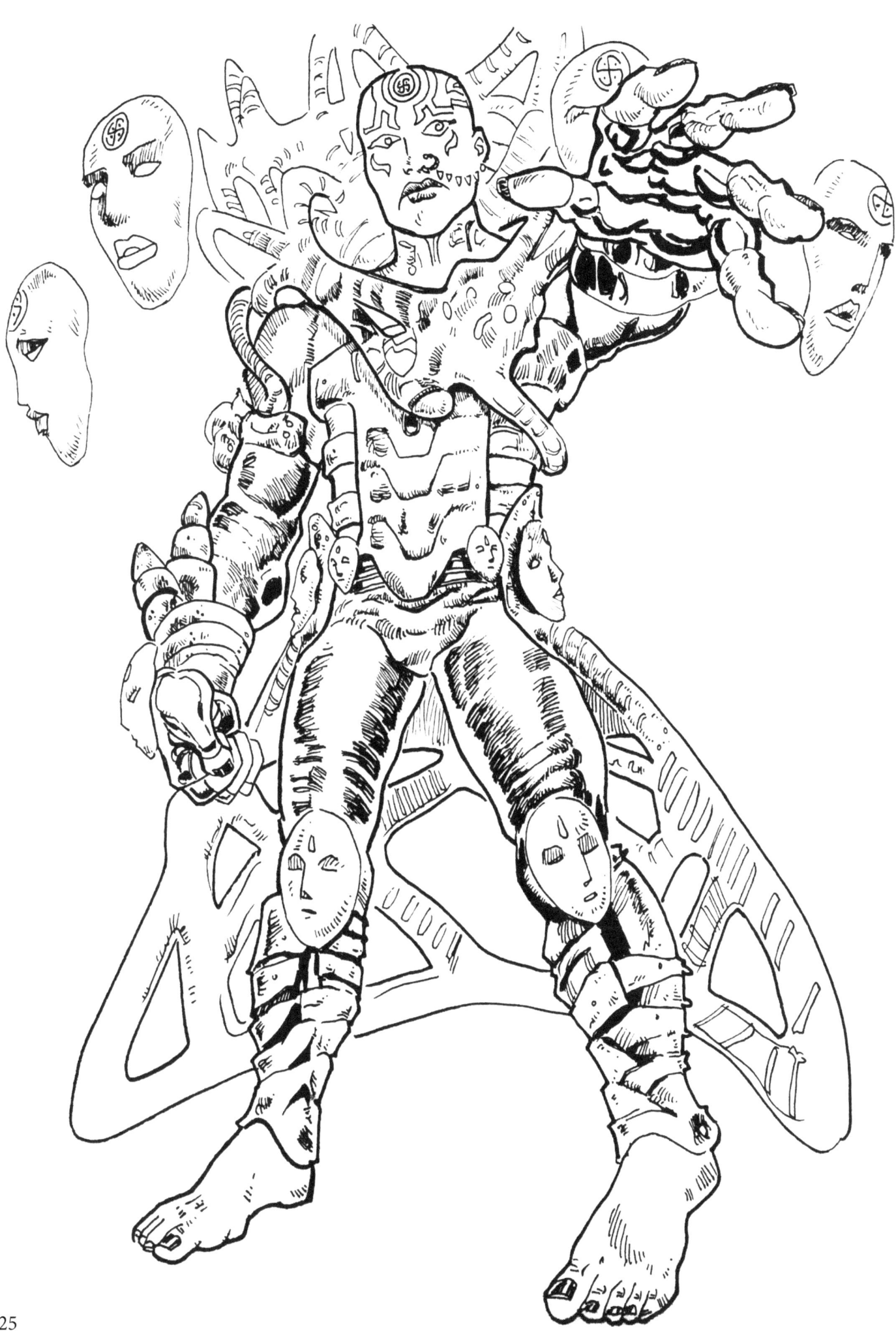

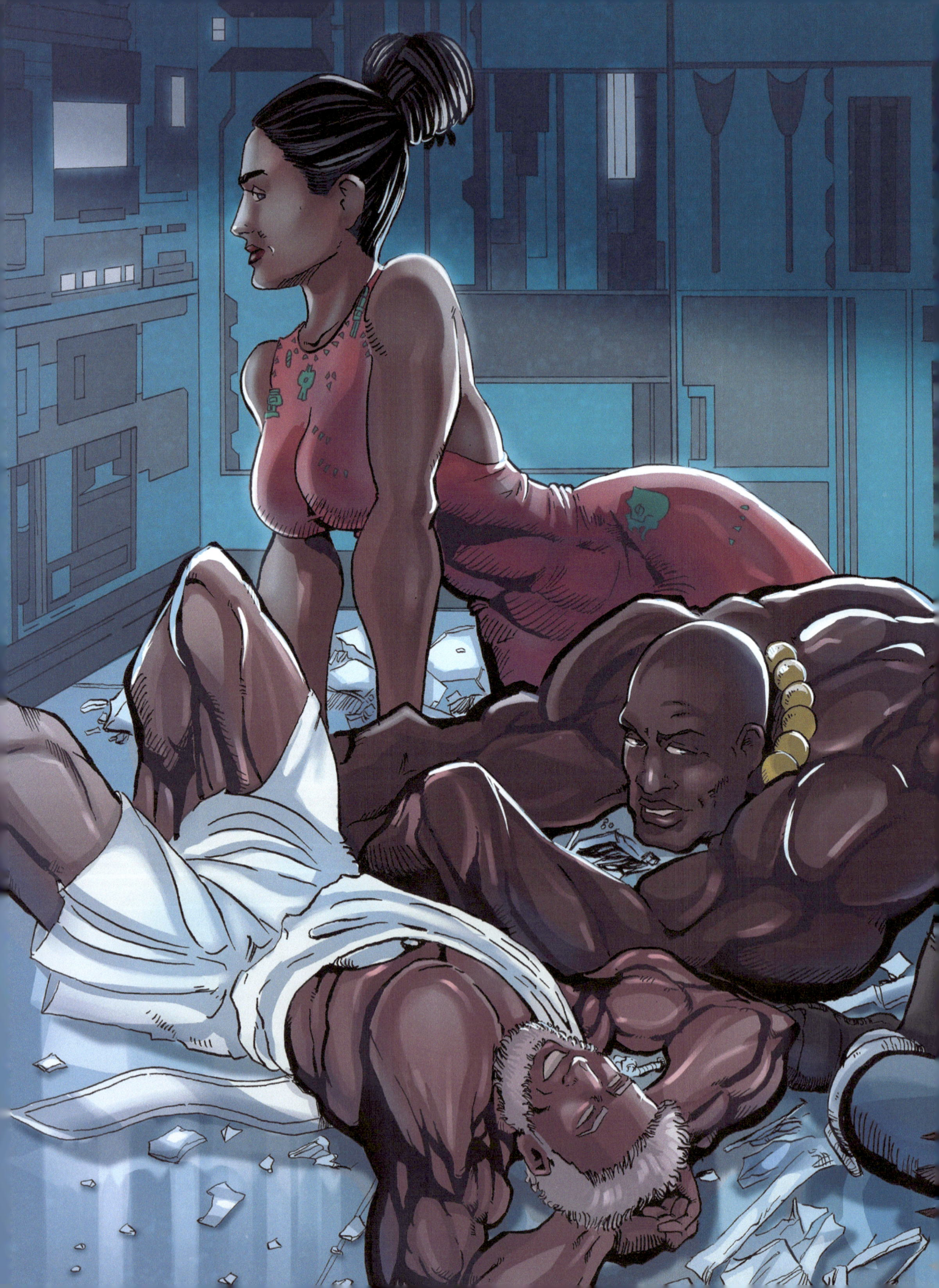

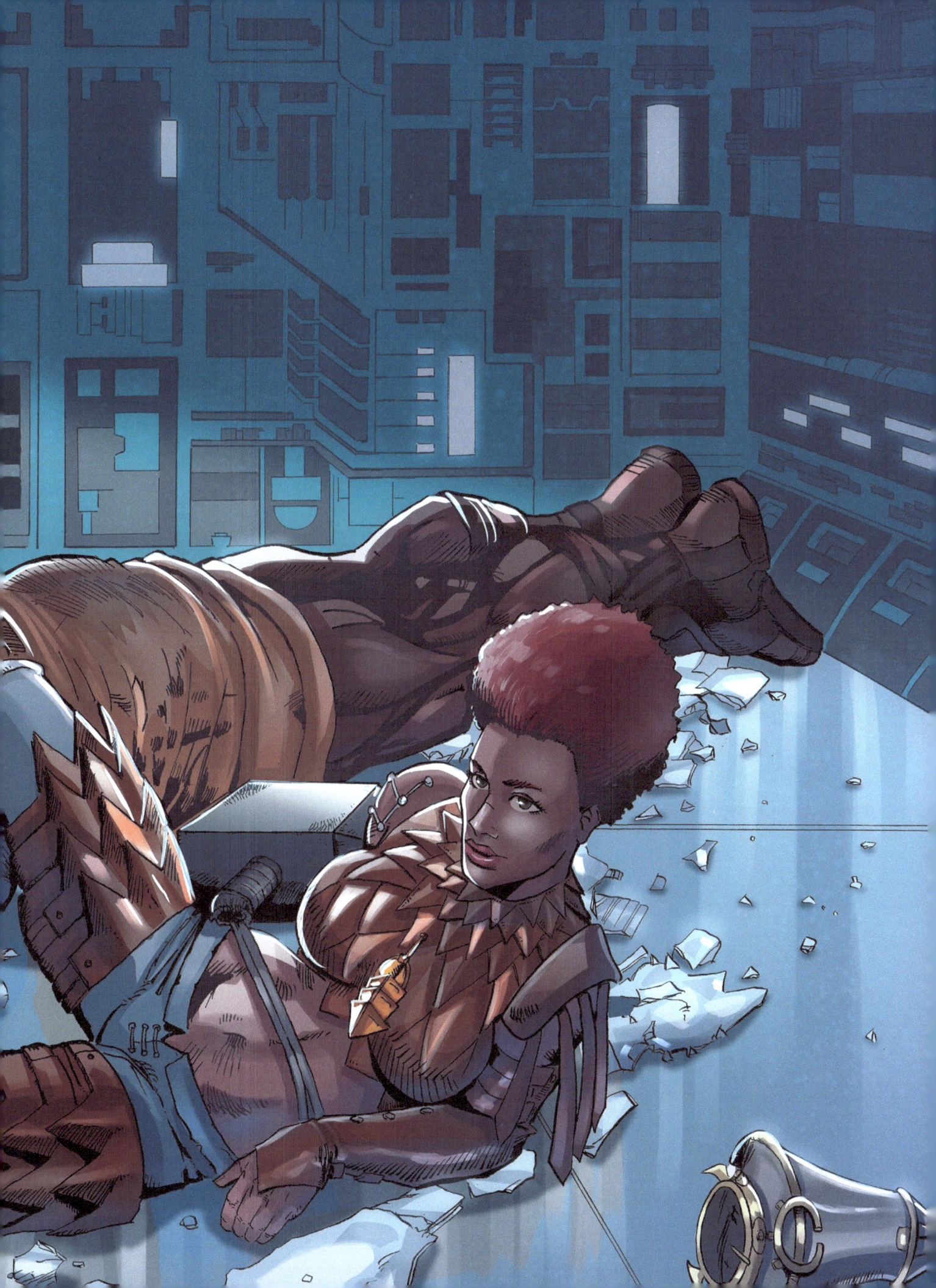

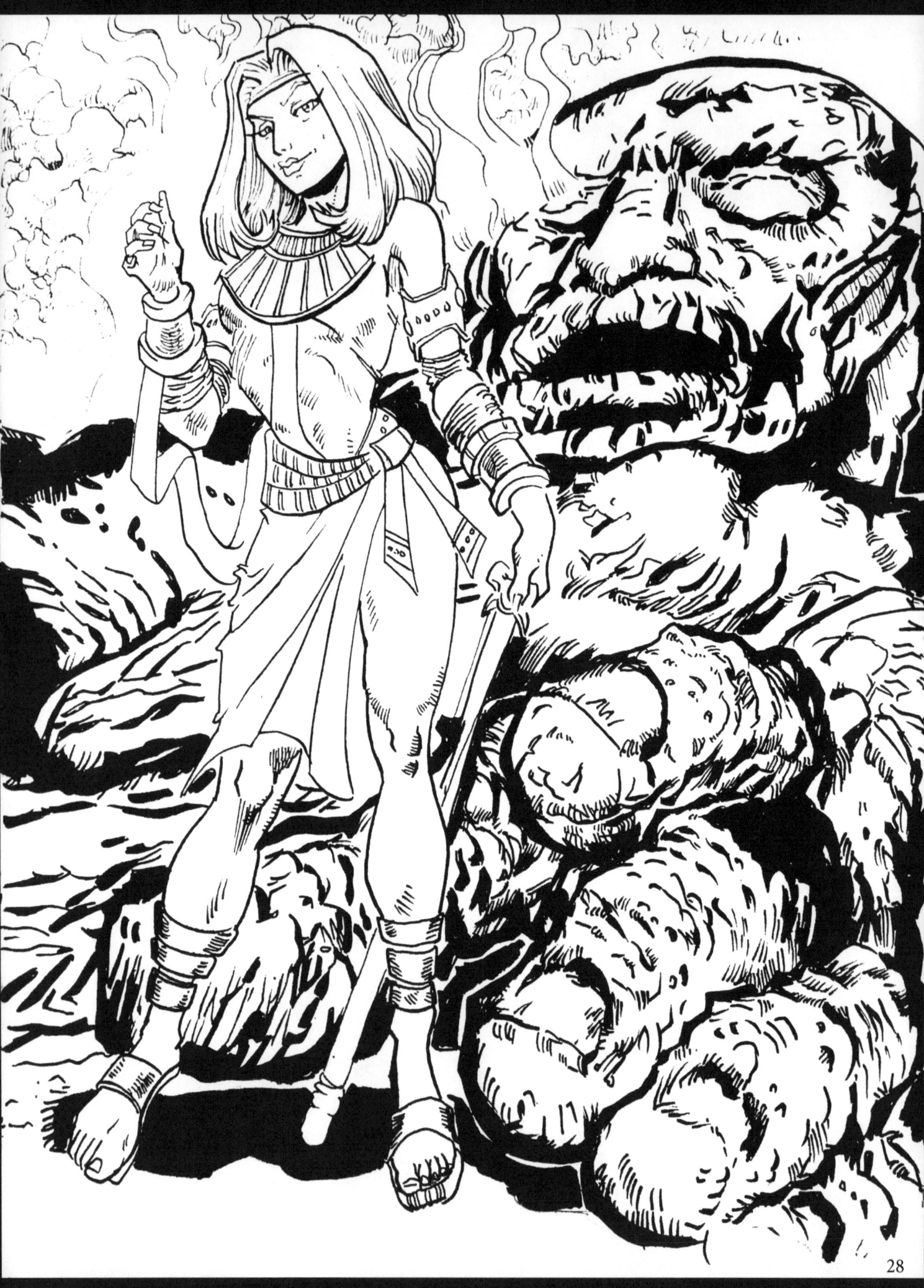

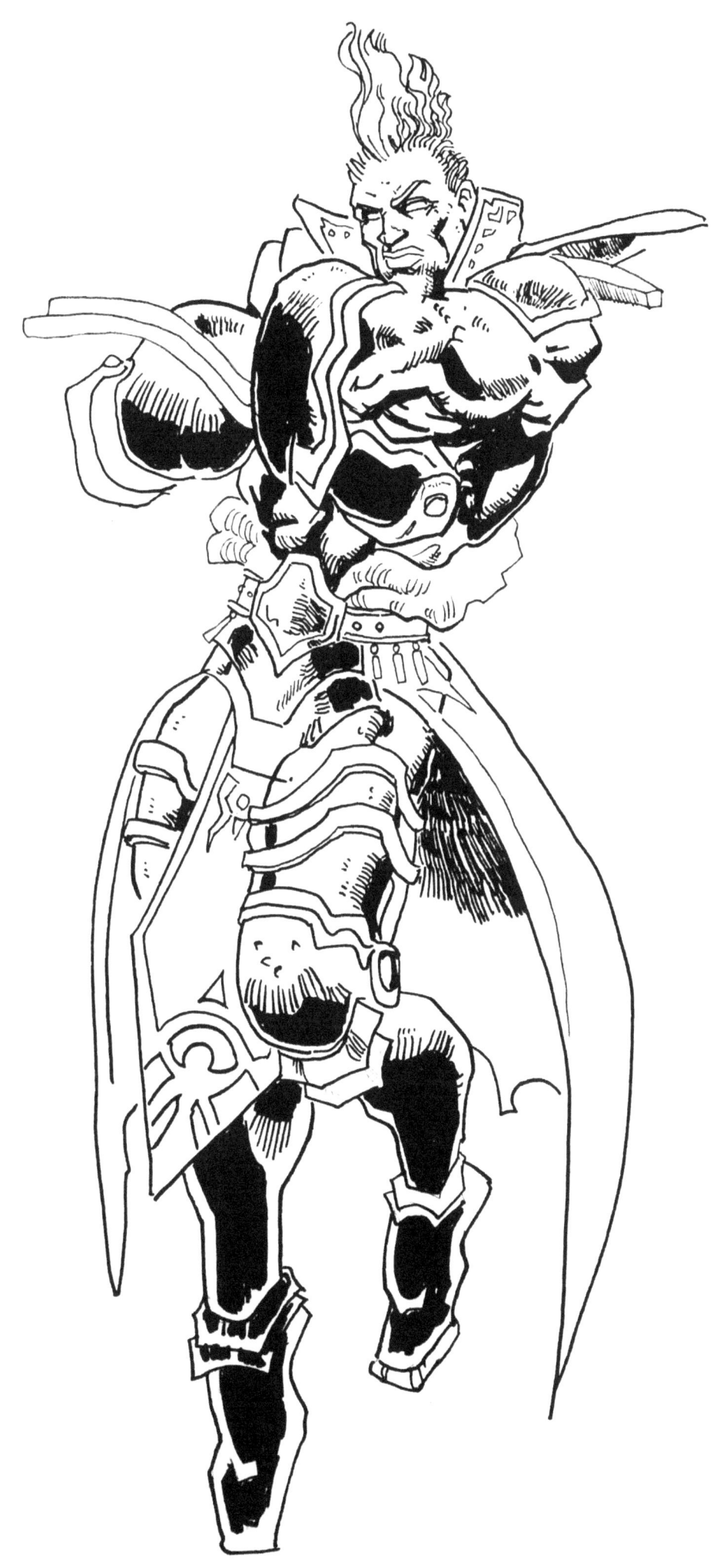

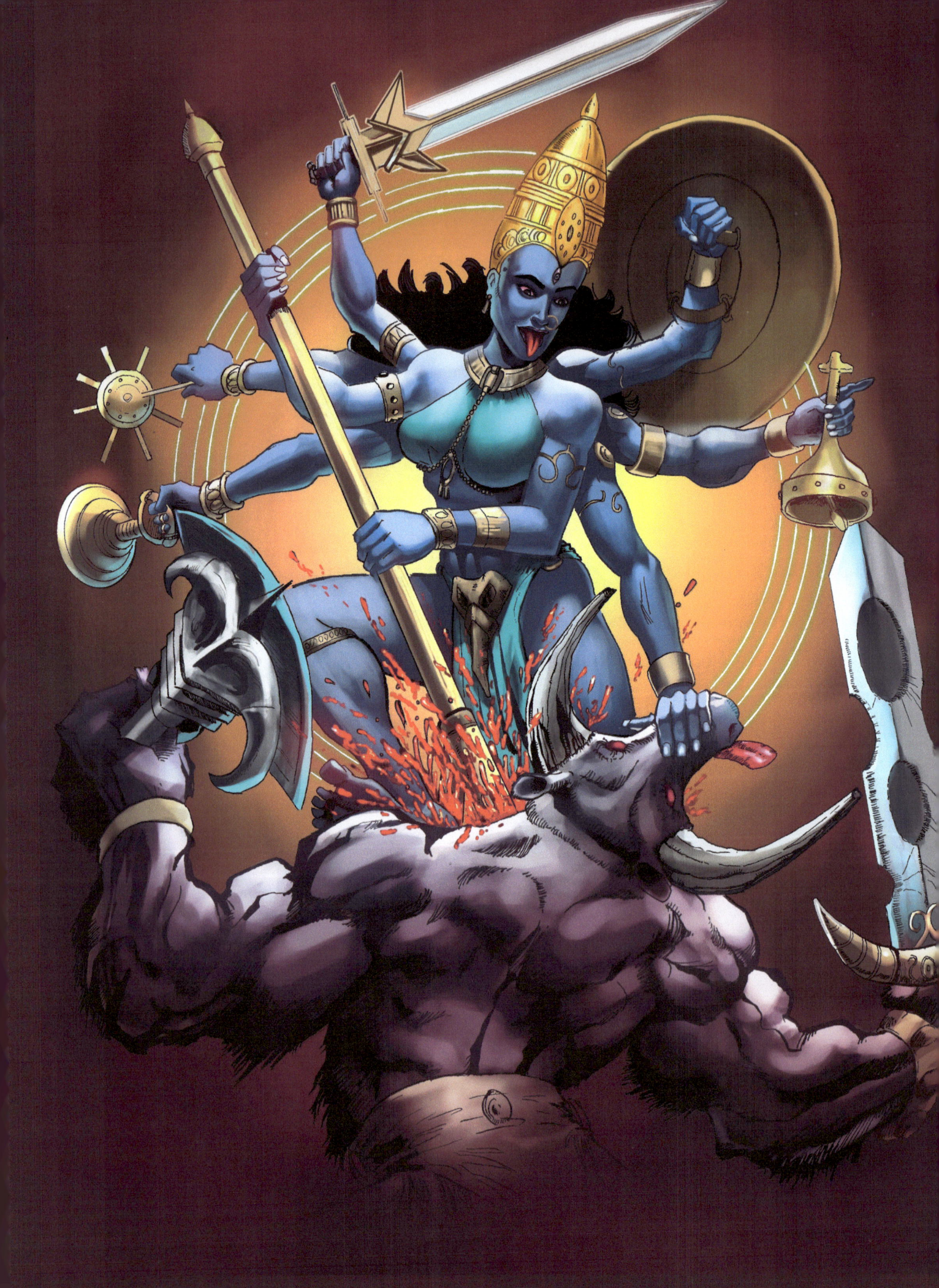

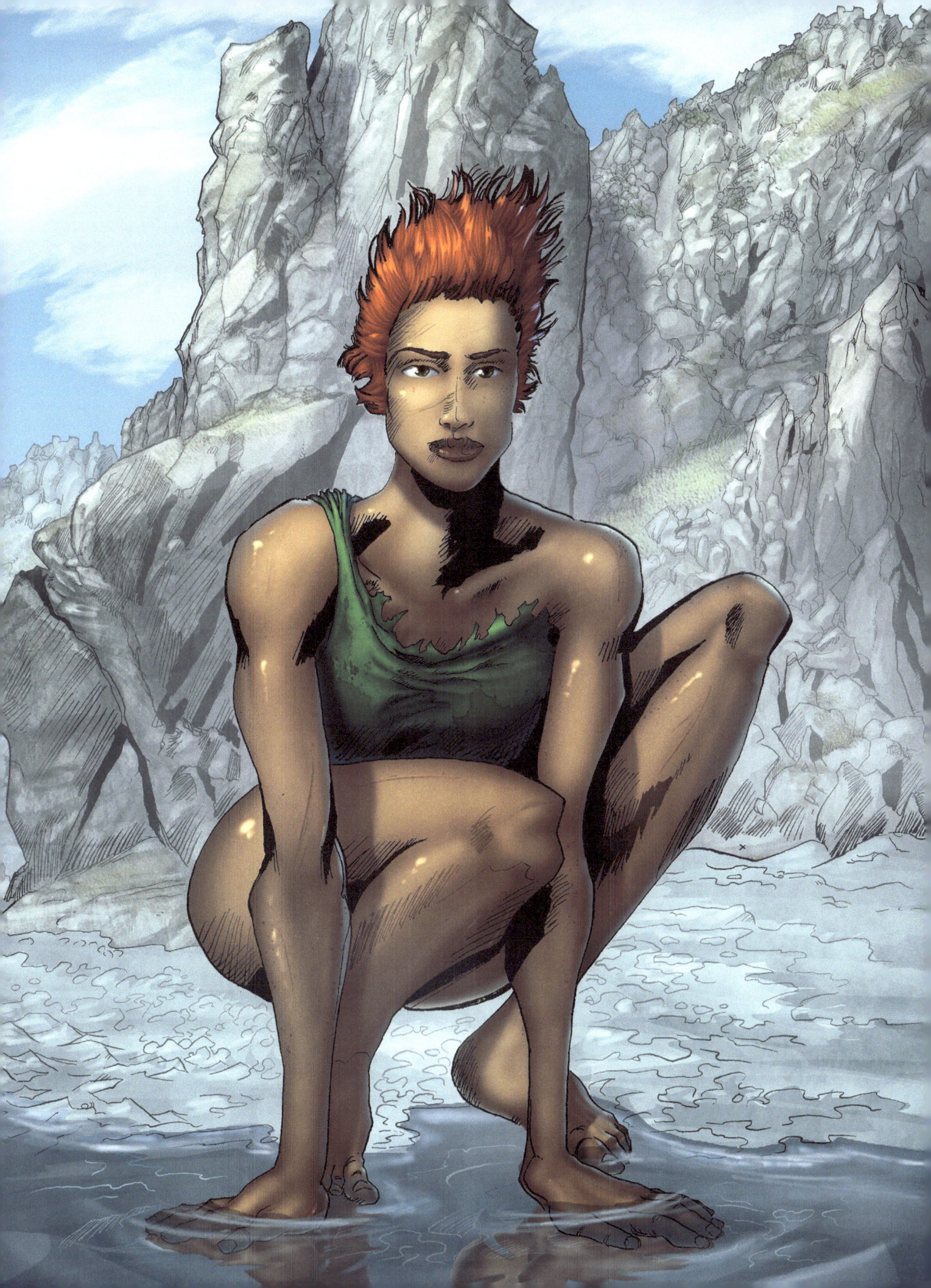

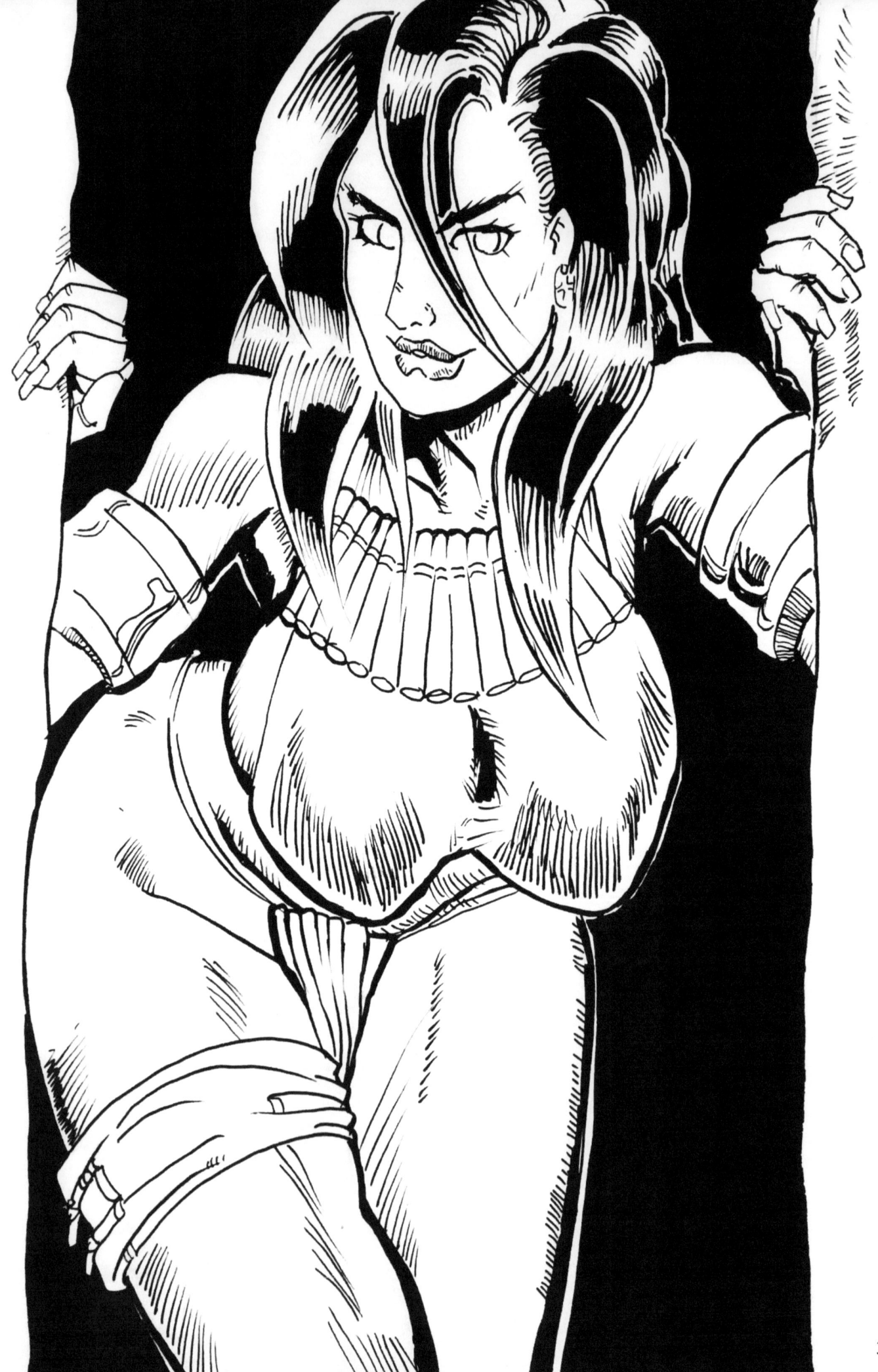

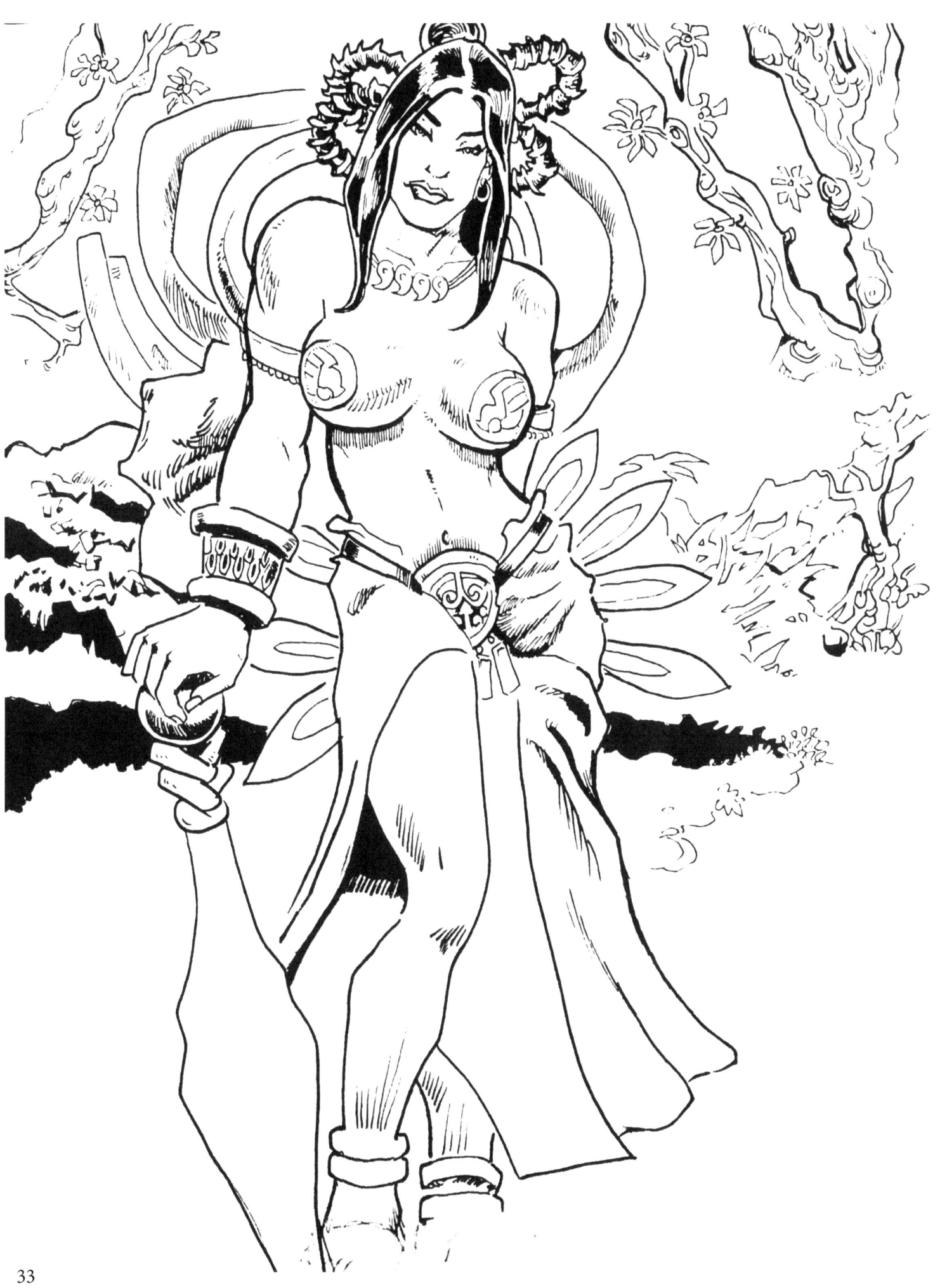

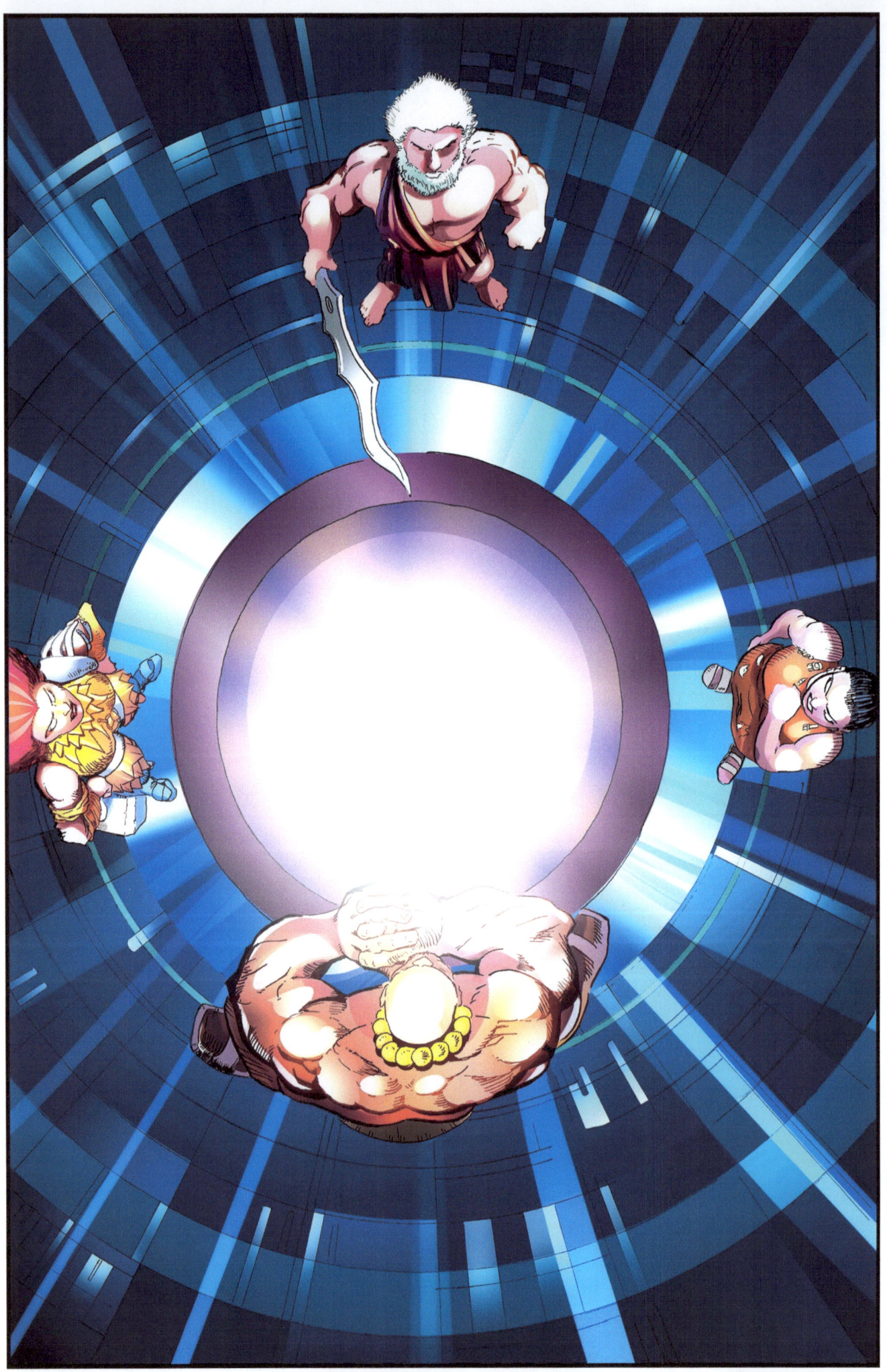

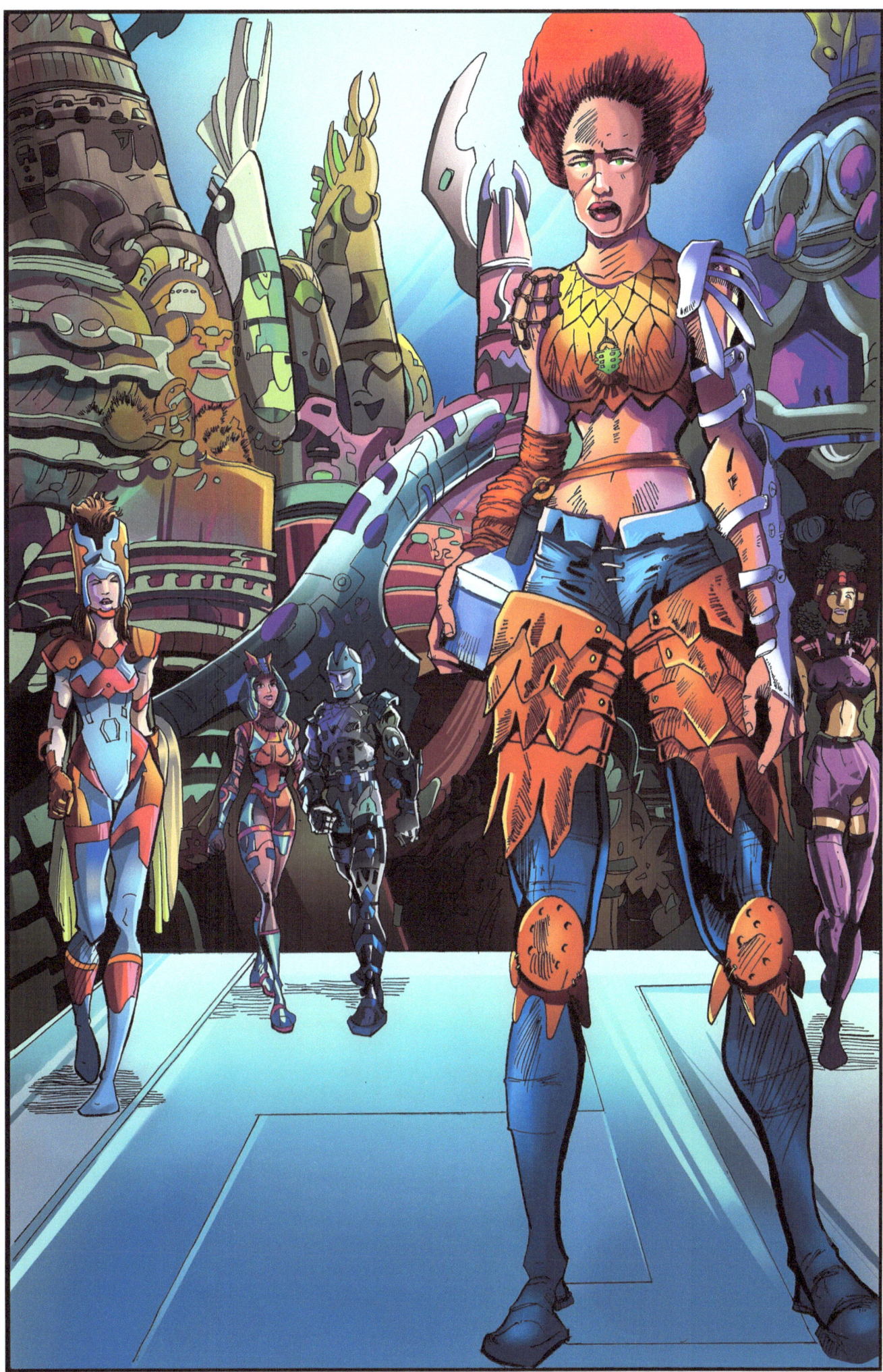

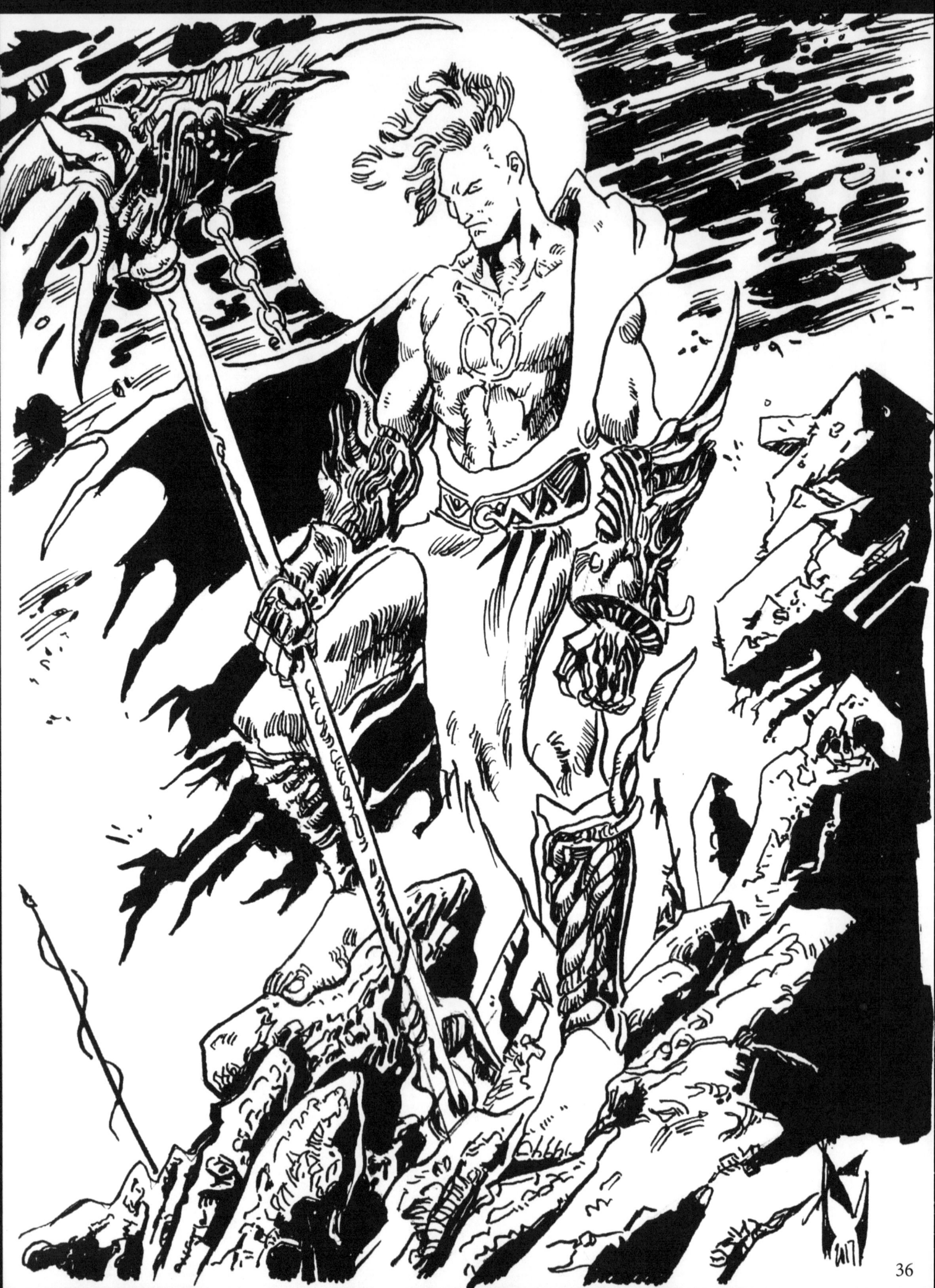

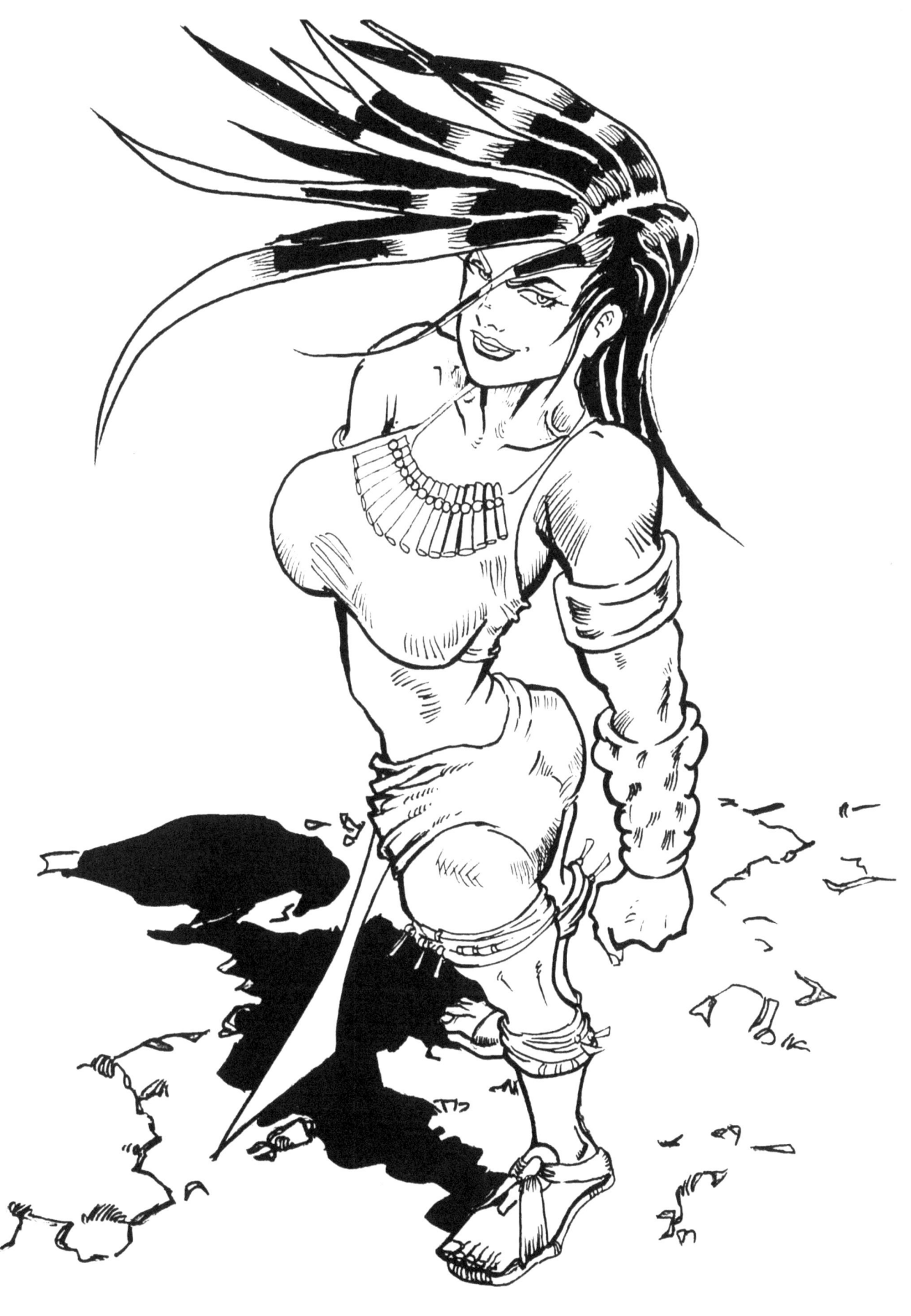

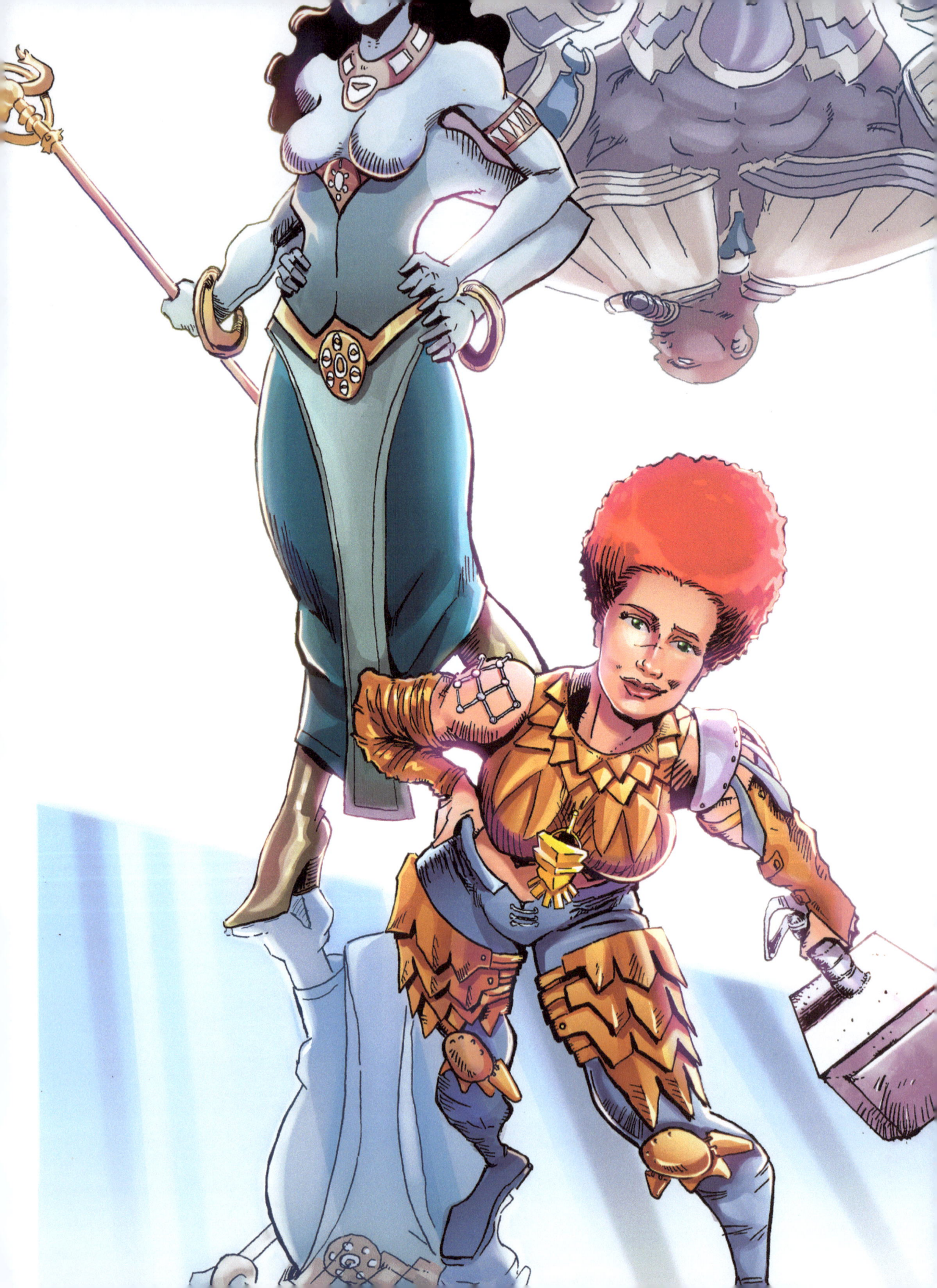

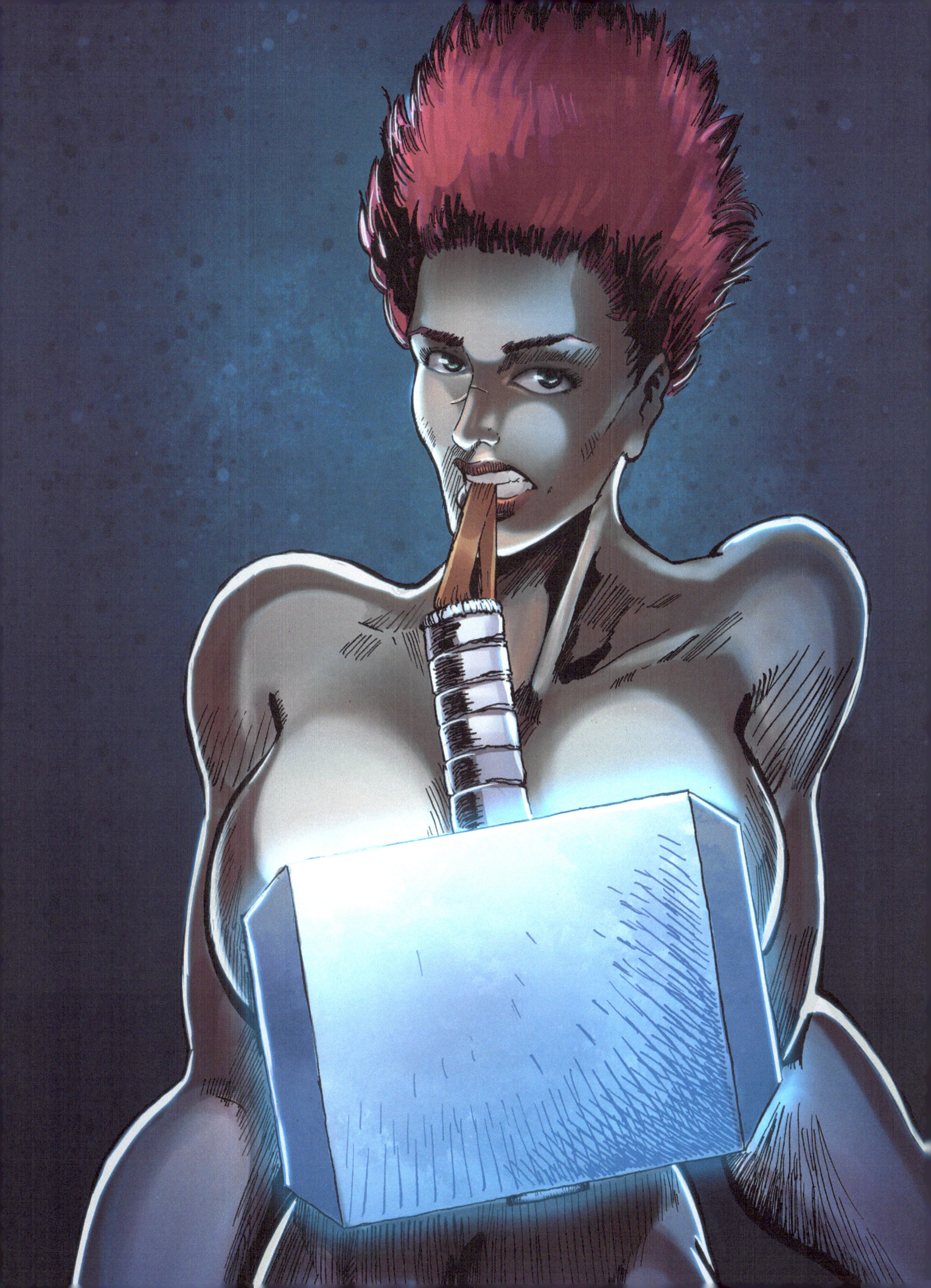

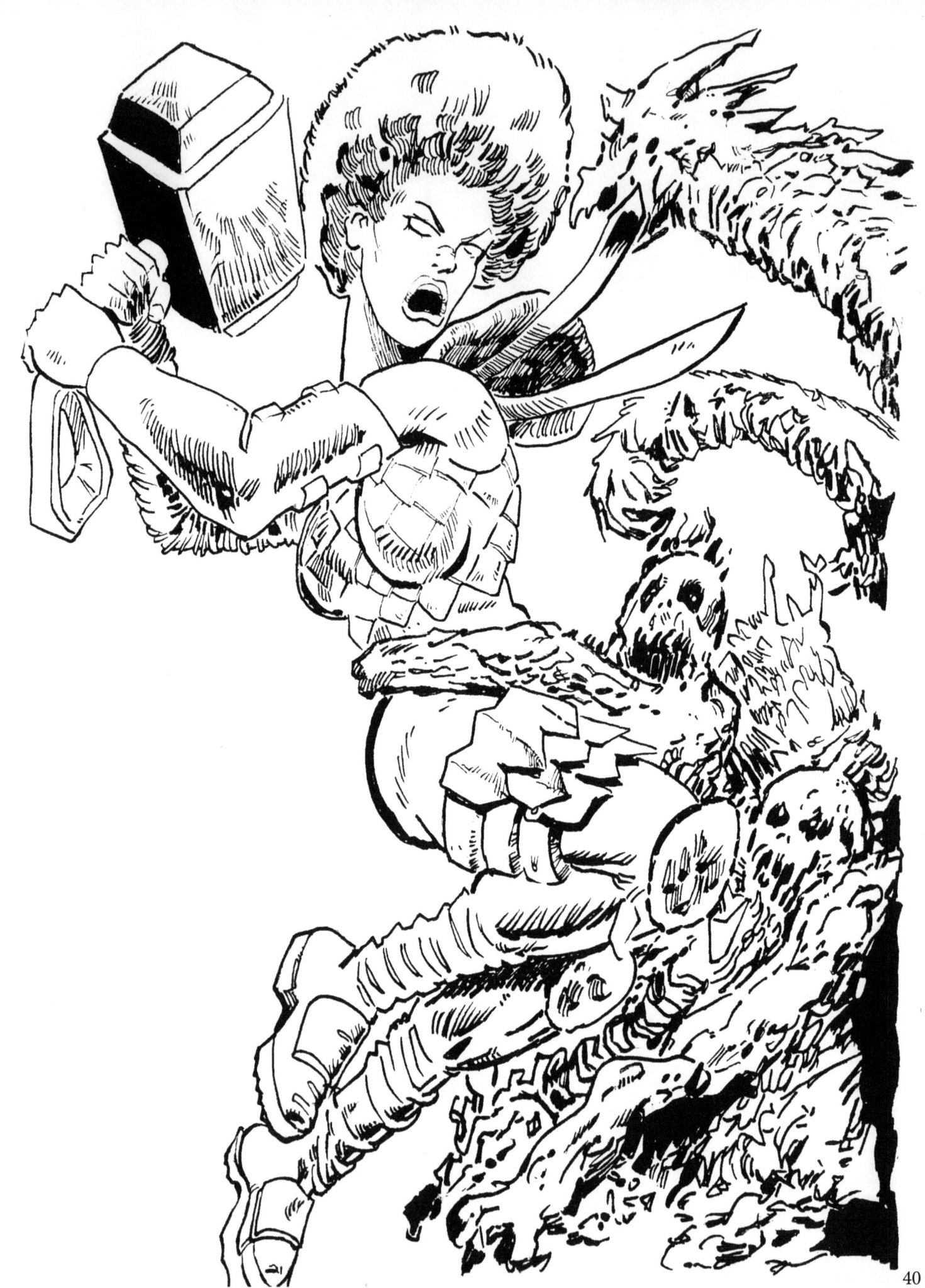

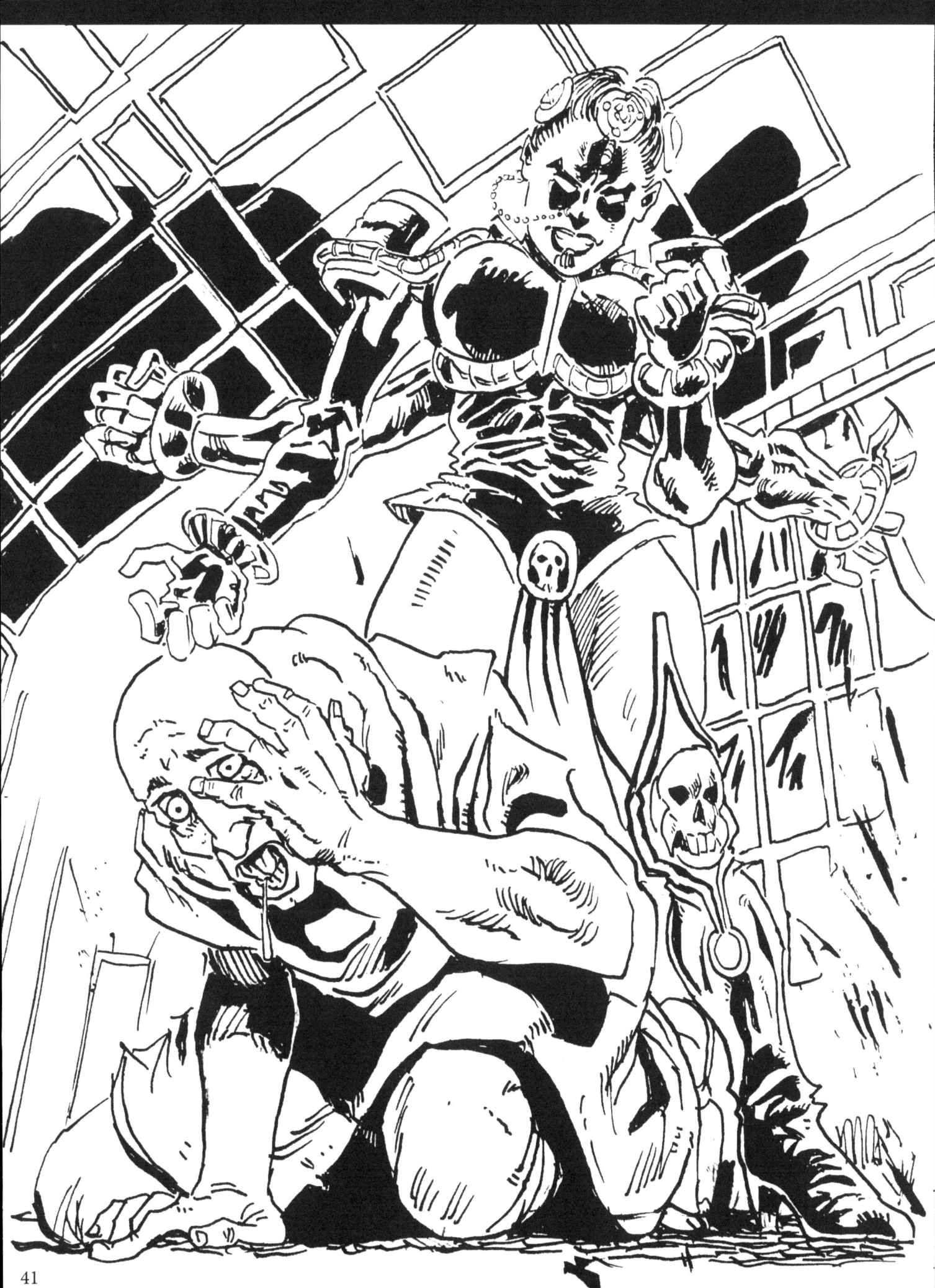

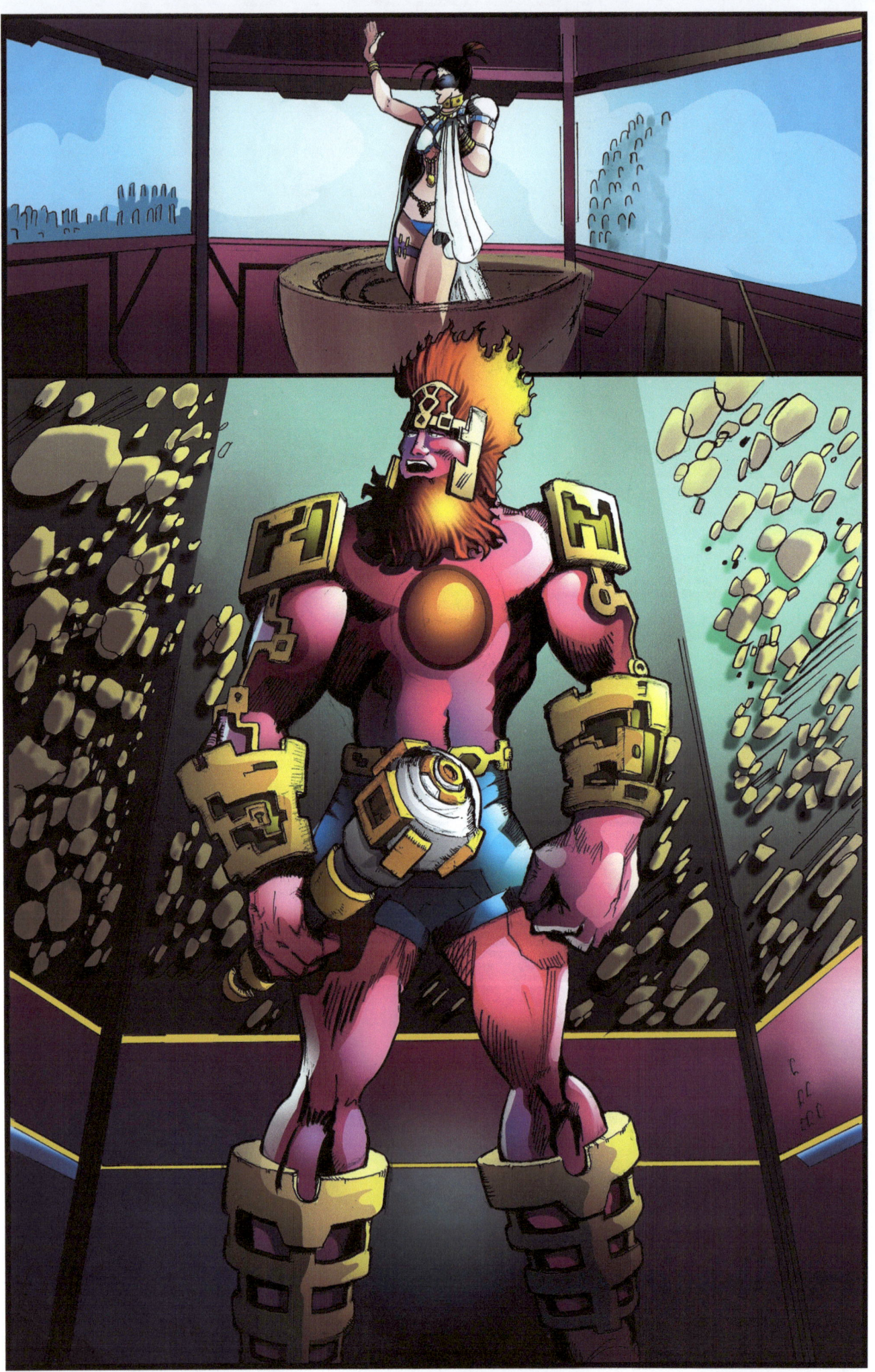

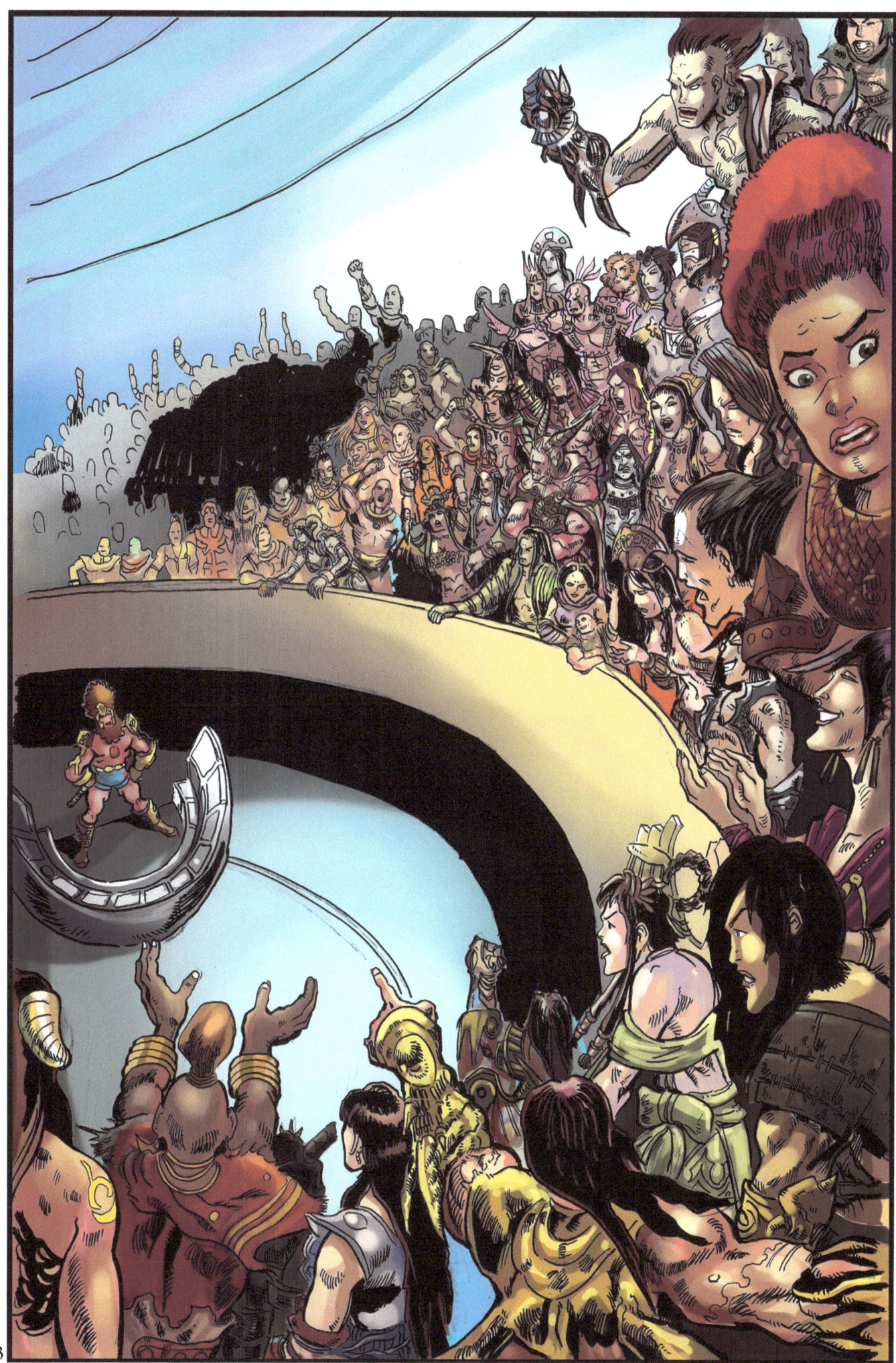

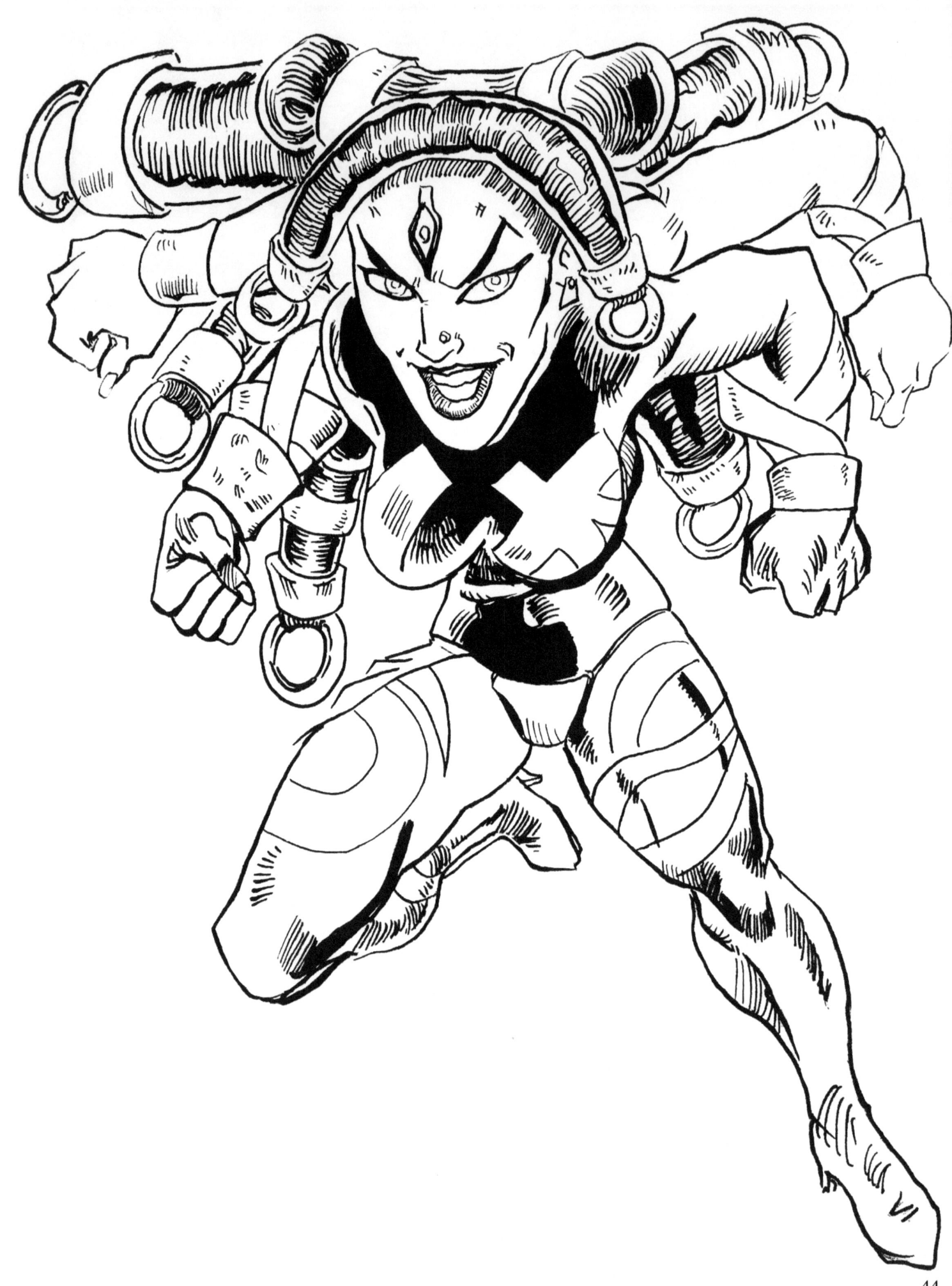

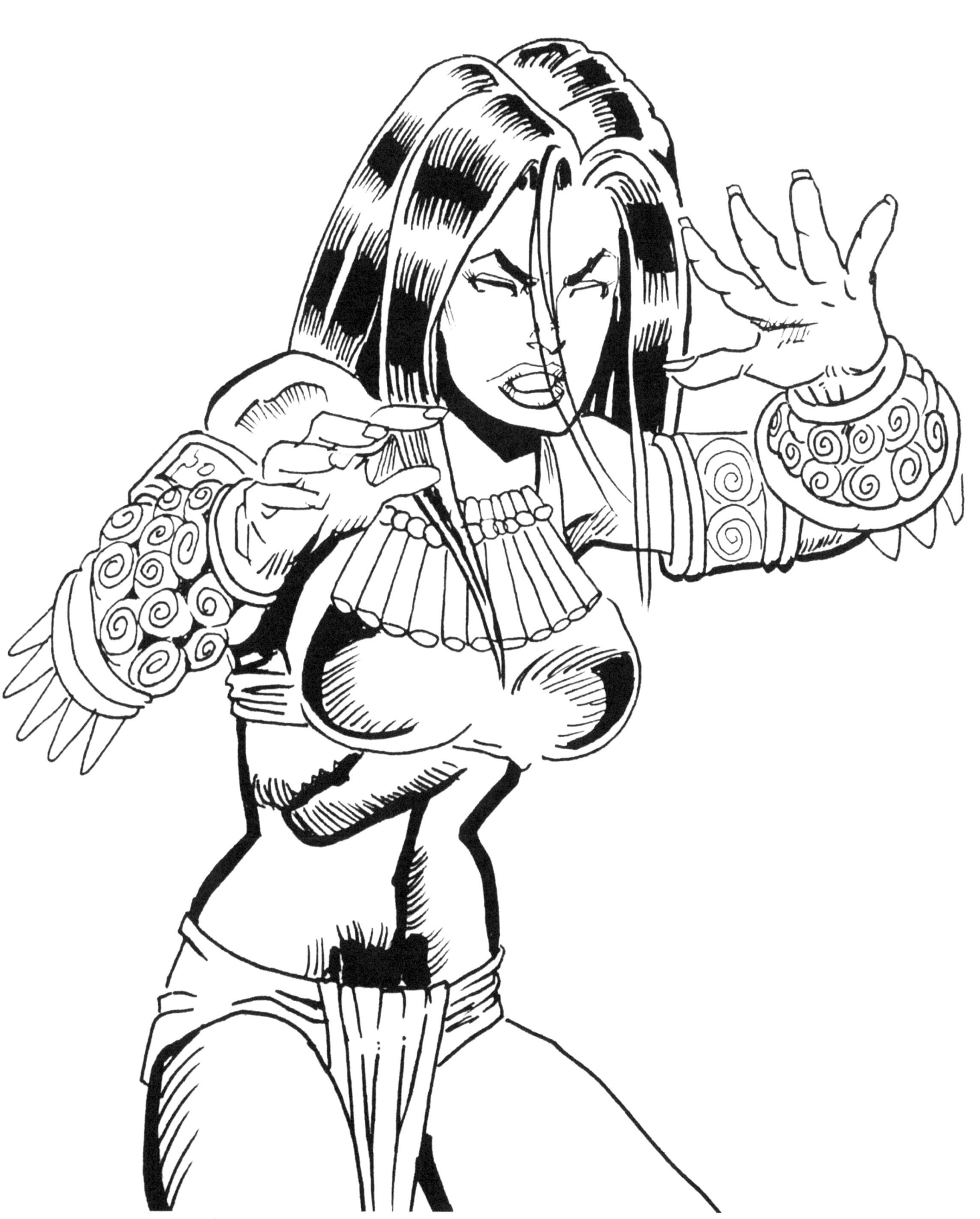

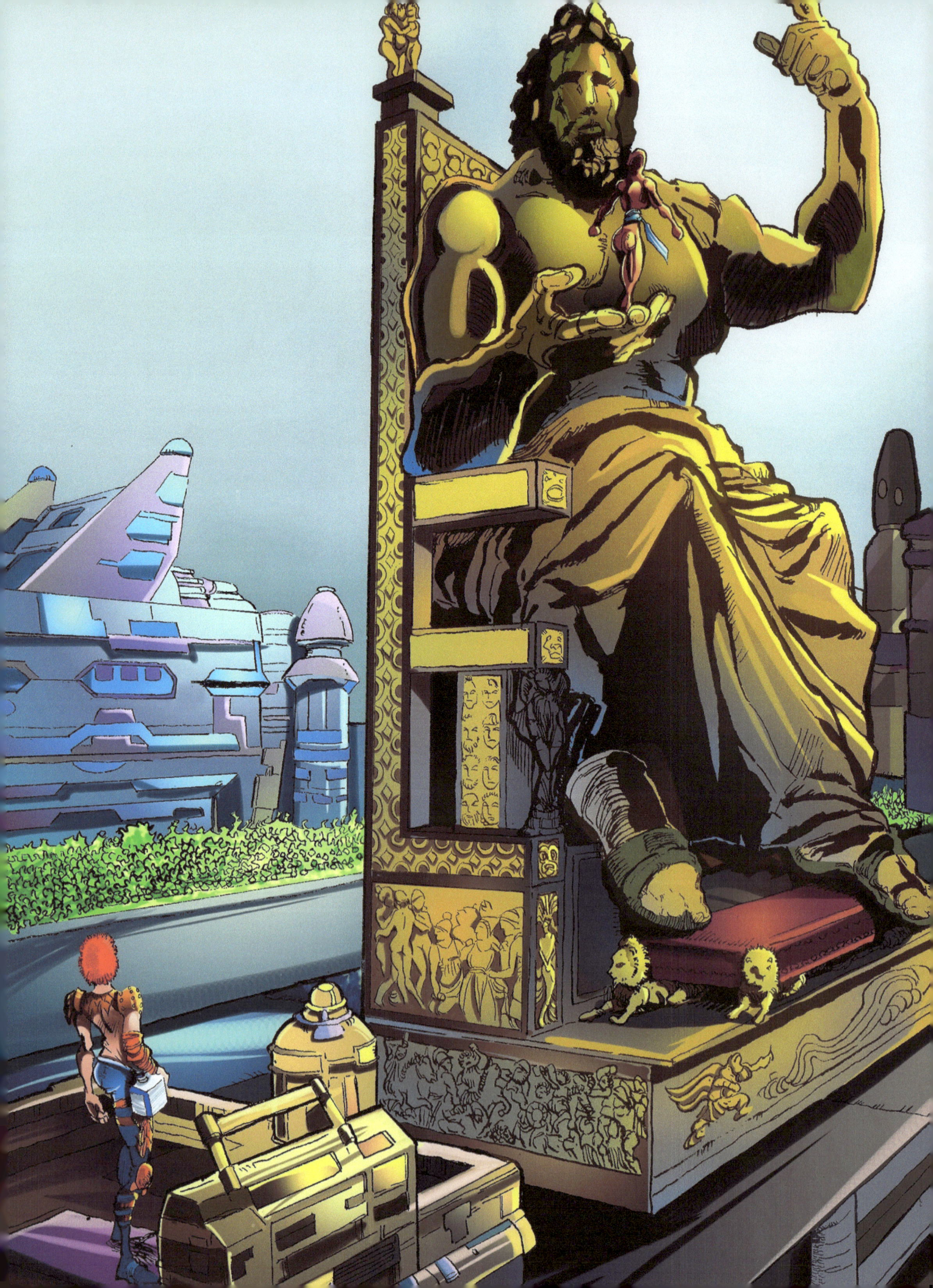

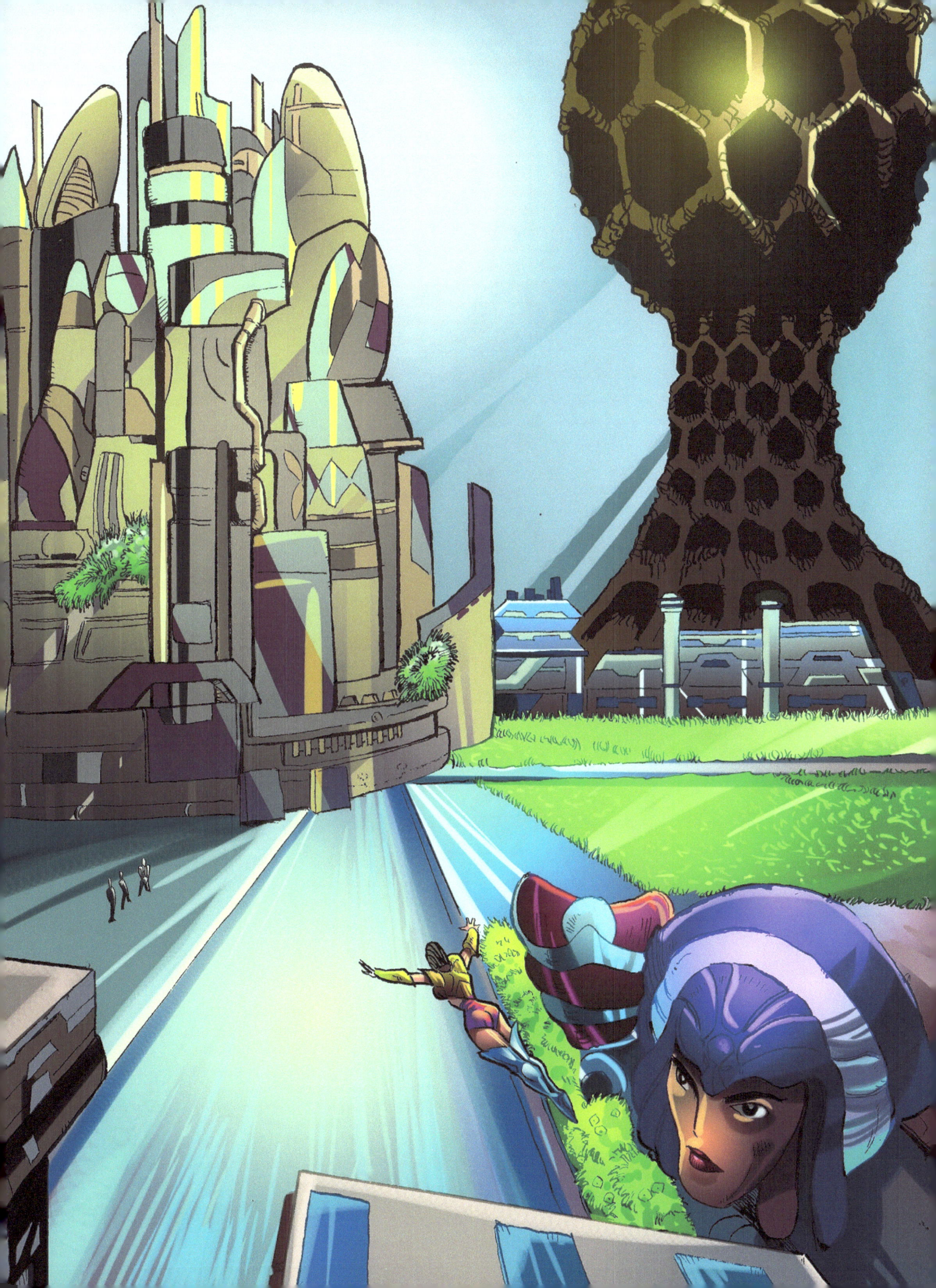

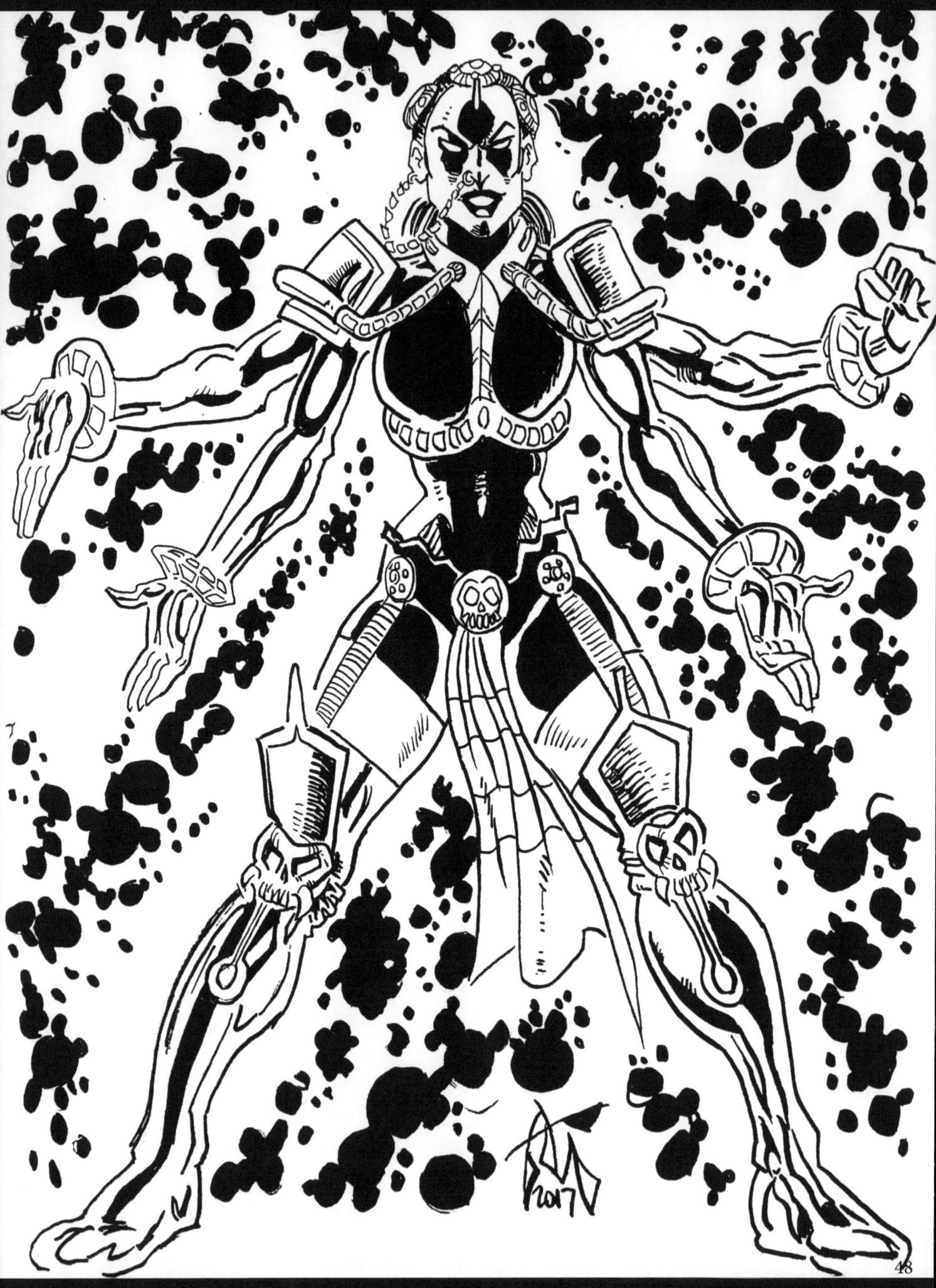

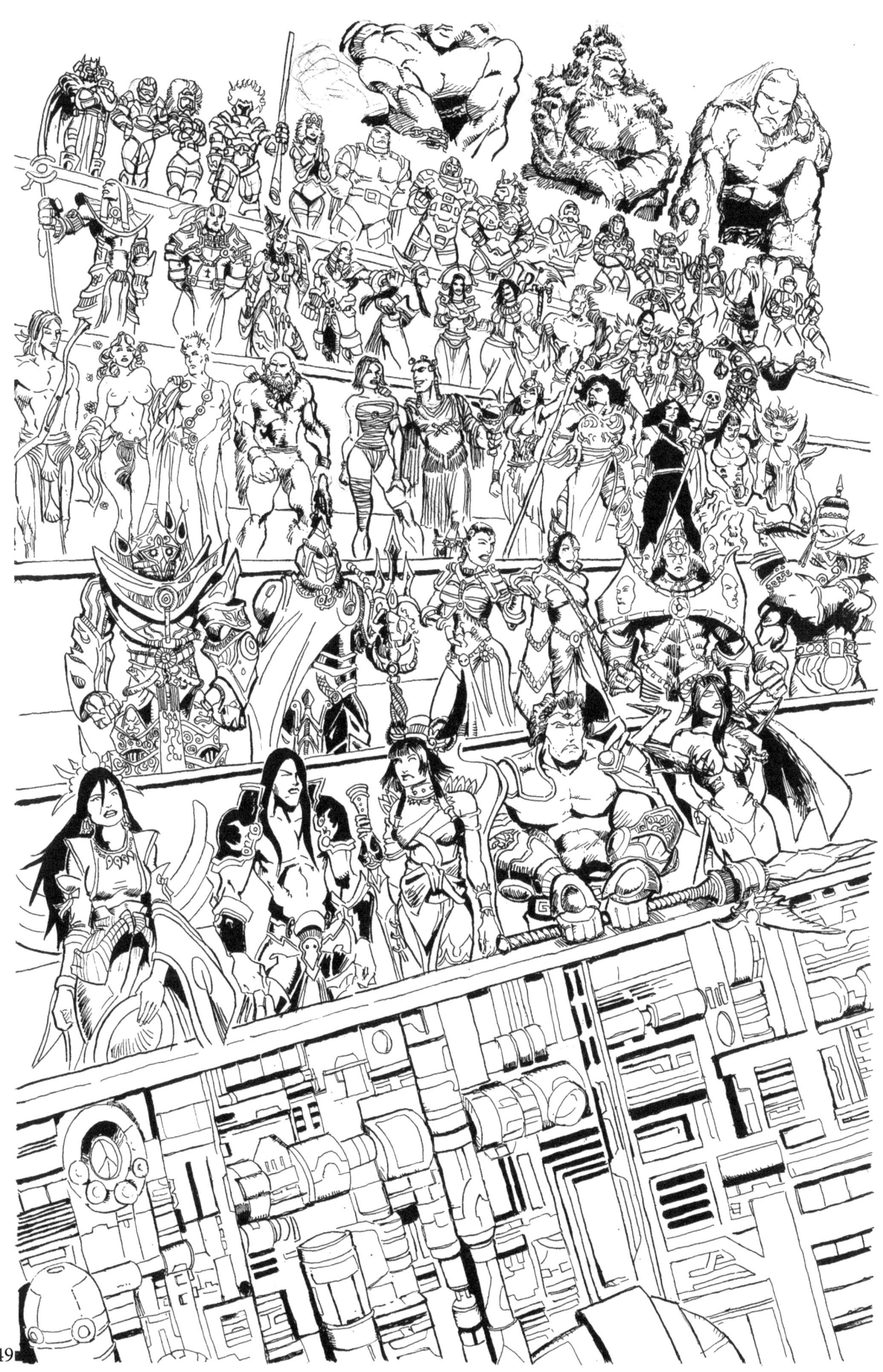

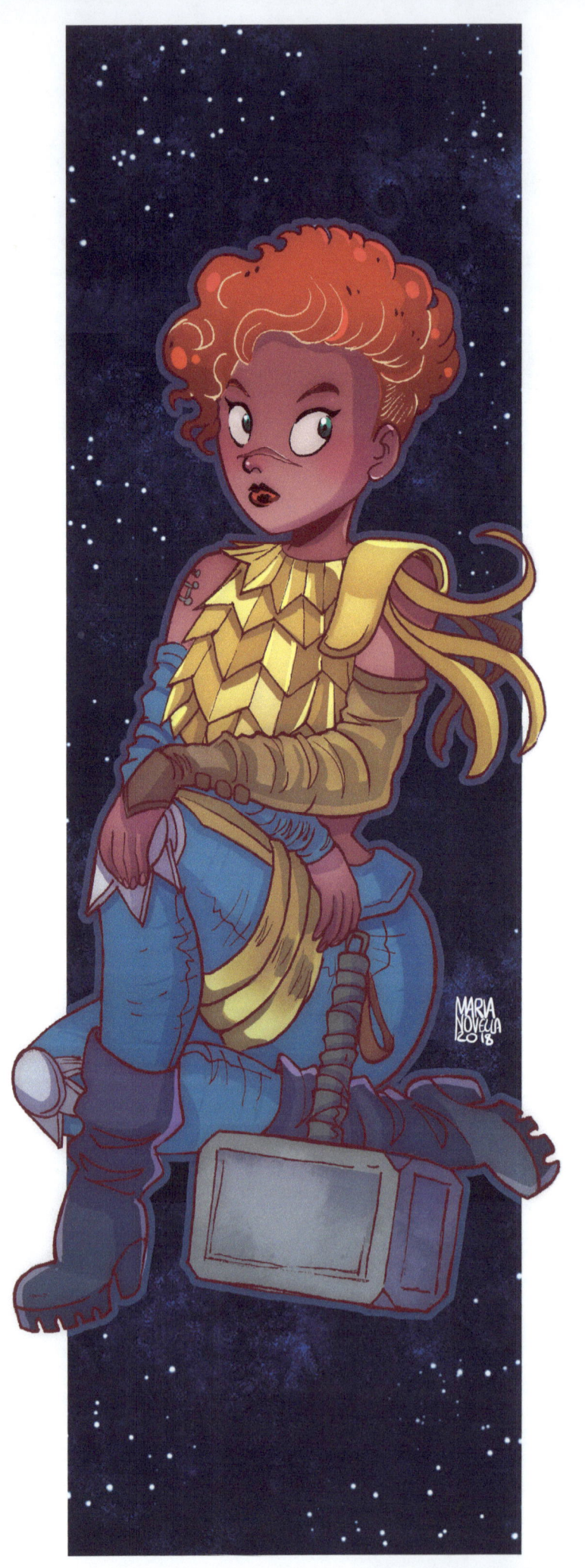

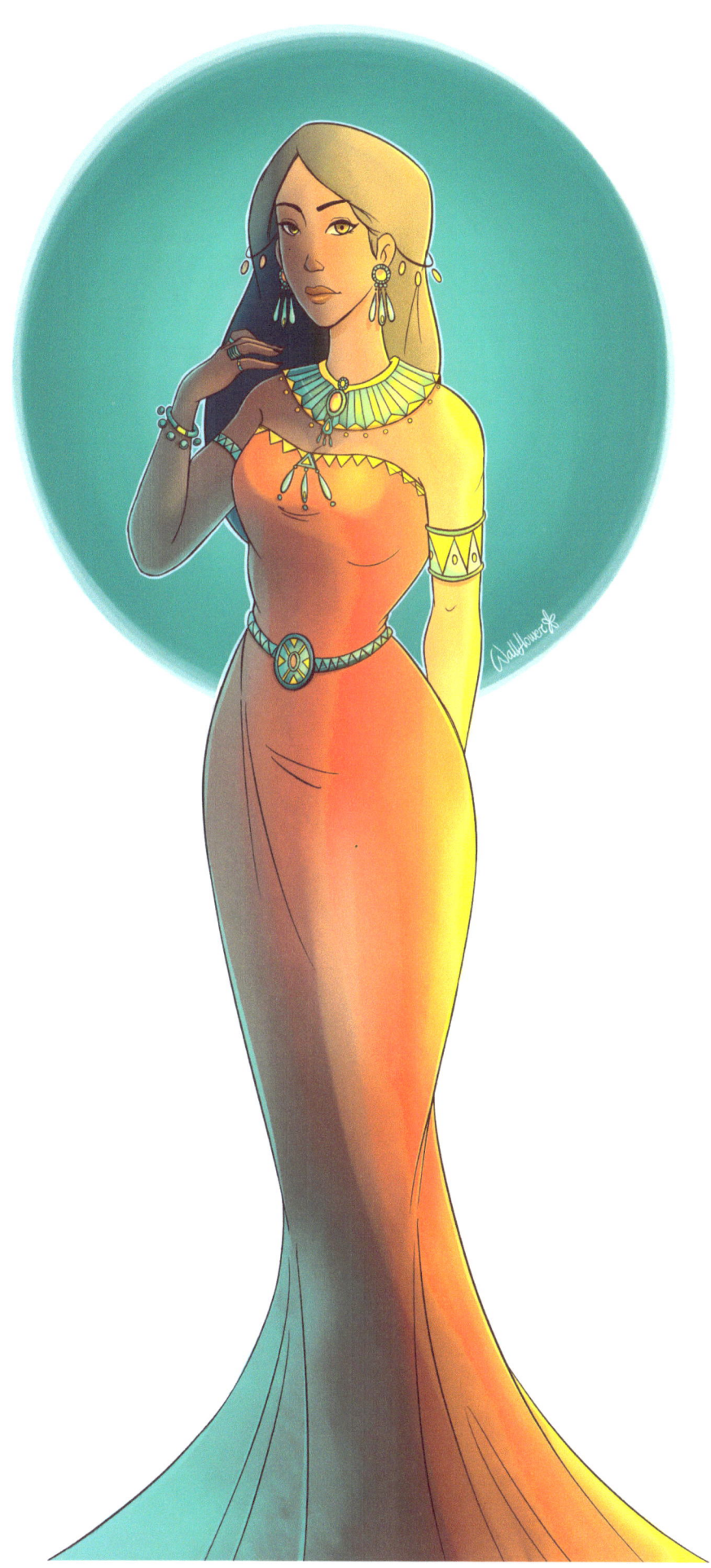

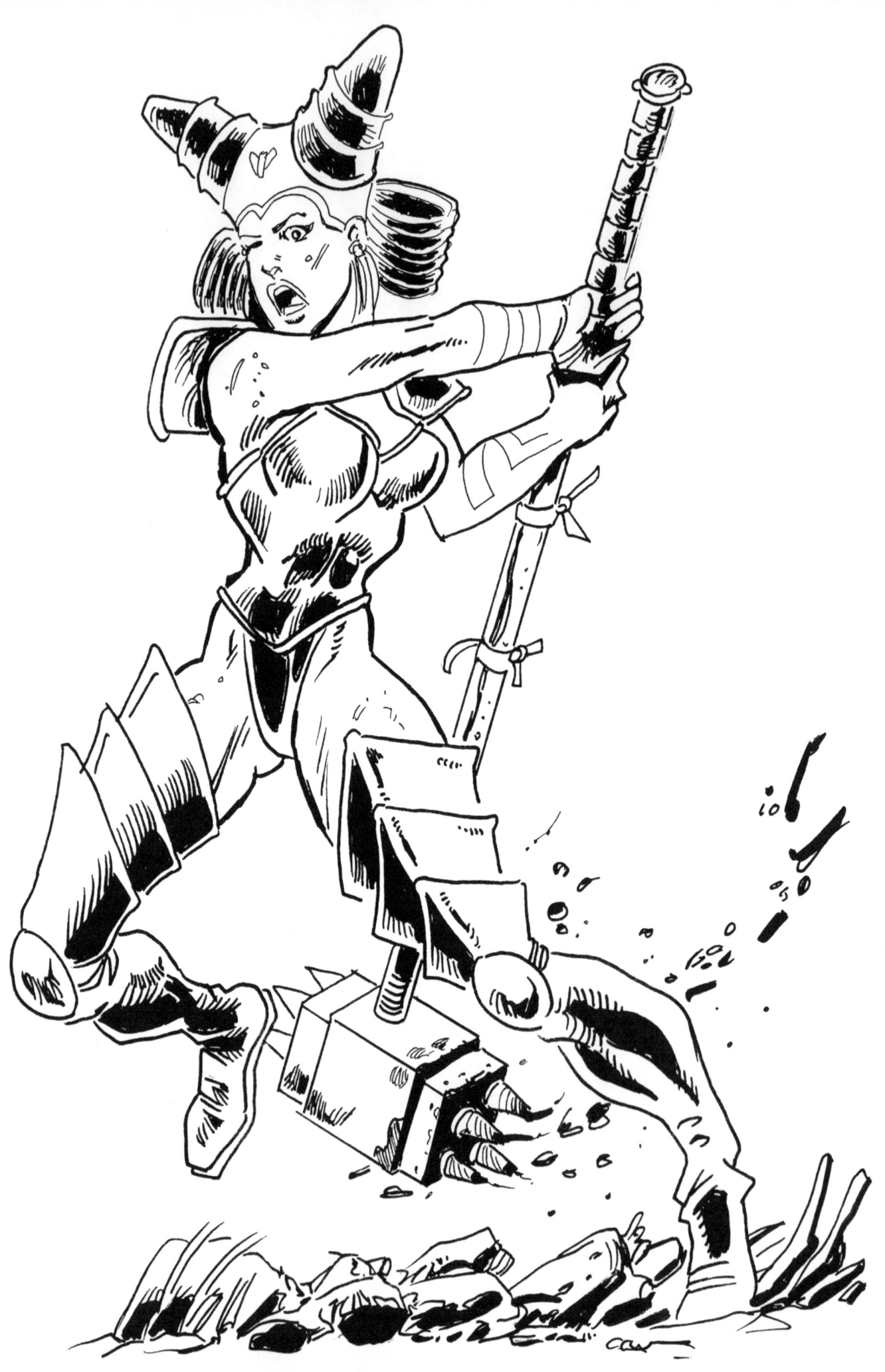

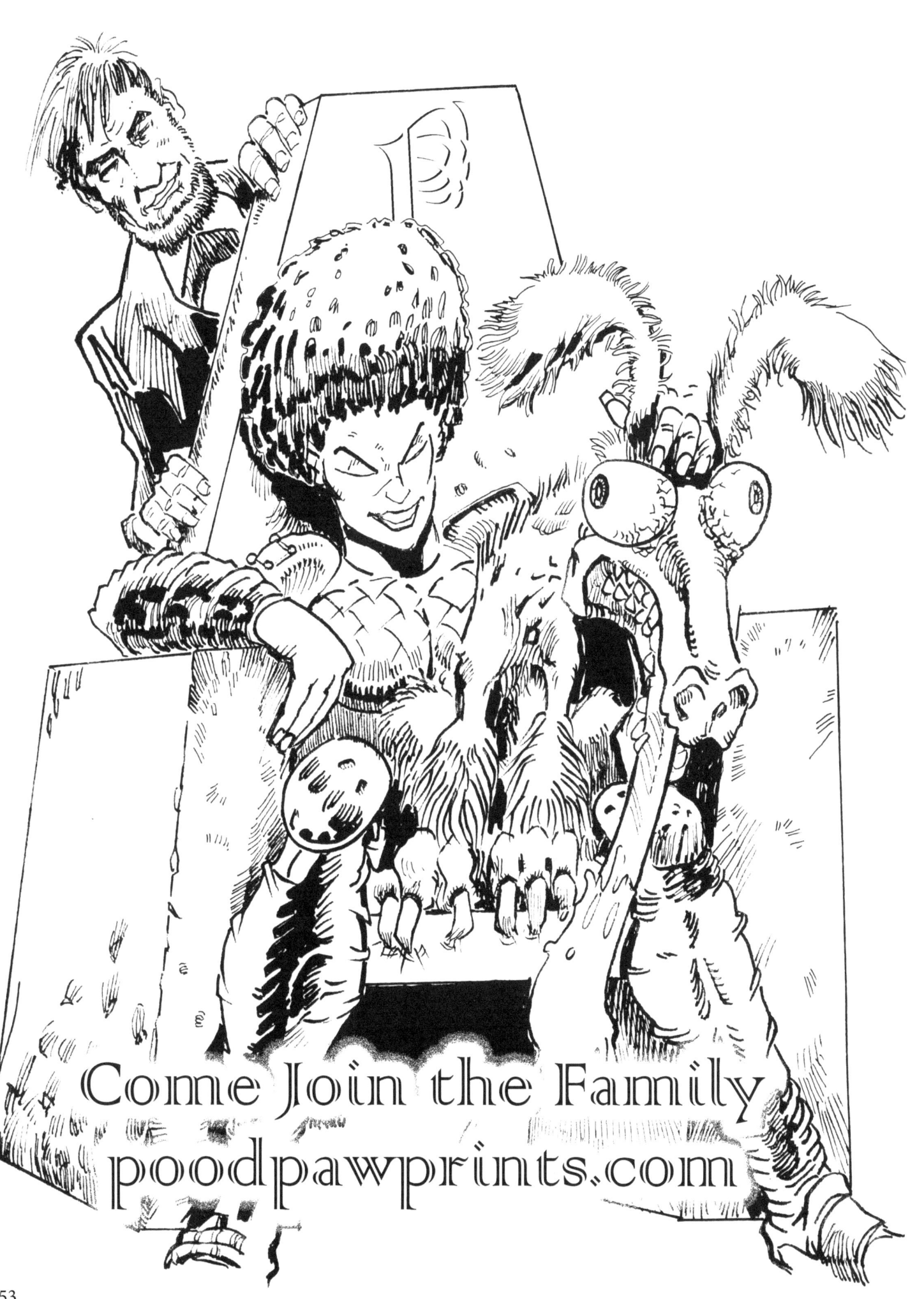

www.ingramcontent.com/pod-product-compliance
Lightning Source LLC
Chambersburg PA
CBHW051218220526
45473CB00003B/1081